# THE LIFE WE WERE MADE FOR

## LEARNING TO LIVE IN THE PRESENCE OF GOD

Brandon D. Arneson

Copyright © 2026 by Brandon D. Arneson
All rights reserved.

No part of this publication may be reproduced, distributed, or transmitted in any form or by any means, including photocopying, recording, or other electronic or mechanical methods, without prior written permission of the publisher, except in the case of brief quotations embodied in reviews and certain other noncommercial uses permitted by copyright law.

Scripture quotations are from the English Standard Version Bible (ESV), unless otherwise noted.

Published independently by Arneson Publishing.

Cover design by Brandon D. Arneson

ISBN: 979-8-234-08317-3

Printed in the United States of America

# Dedication

To my wife, Bethany,
and to our children,

Thank you for sharing this life with me.
For walking through joy and sorrow, faith and uncertainty, calling and sacrifice.
Thank you for your patience, your faithfulness, and your willingness to walk the road of obedience together.

Everything I have built, pursued, and become has been strengthened by your love, your support, and your presence beside me.

You are among God's greatest gifts to me.

And to God,
my Sabbath rest—

Thank You for sustaining me, carrying me, and teaching me that true rest is found not in ease, but in Your presence.

Everything begins and ends with You.

# Table of Contents

# Prologue

## An Invitation to Nearness

There are many ways to live.

Some live hurried. Some live distracted. Some live ambitious. Some live wounded. Many live full lives, but not necessarily formed ones.

We build. We achieve. We strive. We accumulate. We chase meaning through success, relationships, experiences, and possessions, hoping that somewhere in all of it we will find the life we long for.

But often, even after gaining what we wanted, something still feels unfinished. Not because our lives are empty. But because our souls are restless. Deep within every person is a longing that cannot be satisfied by accomplishment, comfort, or control. It is the longing for God. Not merely for His blessings. Not merely for His help.

For Him.

I have spent much of my life in ministry, in missions, and in the care of souls. I have preached in churches, trekked mountain villages, sat in hospital rooms, prayed in moments of breakthrough, and wept in moments of deep uncertainty.

Through all of it, one truth has remained constant: the presence of God changes everything. Not always by changing our circumstances. But by changing us within them.

This book was born out of that conviction. It was forged through sermons preached, prayers prayed, tears shed, and lessons learned—many of them through pain, many through joy, and most through ordinary obedience. These pages are not written from perfection. They are written from pursuit.

I have not mastered the presence of God. But I have learned that the life we were made for is not found in what we accomplish for God, but in learning to live with Him.

That is the invitation of this book.

Not to perform. Not to pretend. Not to become religious. But to become present. To wake up to the God who is nearer than you know. To learn His voice. To reorder your life around His nearness. To become the kind of person who walks with God in ordinary life. Because the greatest gift God gives is not merely direction, peace, provision, or purpose.

It is Himself.

And if that is true, then the best life available to us is the life lived in His presence. This is the life we were made for.

As you pursue the presence of God, May the LORD bless you and keep you. May He cause His face to shine upon you.

May YAHWEH lift His countenance upon you and gift your soul with His presence and peace. In the Name that is above every other name, Jesus, Amen.

— **Brandon D. Arneson**

# Introduction
# The Life We Were Made For

As one entrusted with the care of human souls, I often find myself returning to the same question: **How do I help people experience the life God truly intends for them?**

Not mere survival. Not religious performance. Not simply enduring the day. But genuine spiritual vitality. A flourishing life. A life shaped by the nearness of God.

As a pastor, missionary, husband, and father, I have spent years walking with people through both the beauty and brokenness of life. I have stood beside hospital beds, prayed through family crises, navigated ministry in hostile environments, and wrestled through seasons of fear, pain, uncertainty, and surrender in my own life.

And through all of it, one truth has become increasingly clear:

**The best life God has for us is not found in comfort, success, or ease. It is found in His presence.**

That may sound simple. But it is not shallow. The presence of God is not a sentimental idea or an abstract theological concept. It is the very environment for which humanity was created. At the center of the biblical story is not merely morality, mission, or even redemption itself, but communion.

Scripture tells one unfolding story: **God desires to dwell with His people.**

In Genesis, humanity begins in the presence of God. Adam and Eve walked with Him in the garden in unhindered fellowship. There was no separation. No shame. No hiding. Humanity's first home was the presence of God.

But sin fractured that communion. What was once natural became distant. What was once intimate became interrupted. And from that moment forward, the story of Scripture becomes the story of God moving toward His people.

In Exodus, God localized His presence in the tabernacle, dwelling in the midst of Israel as they wandered through the wilderness. In the temple, His glory rested among His covenant people as a visible reminder that He had not abandoned them.

Then, in John, something extraordinary happened. God took on flesh. Jesus Christ became the embodied presence of God among humanity. John tells us that "the Word became flesh and dwelt among us." The word *dwelt* literally carries the idea of "tabernacled." God moved into the neighborhood. And through Christ, access was restored.

Then in Acts, the Holy Spirit was poured out—not merely visiting God's people, but indwelling them. What was once external became internal. What was once visited became inhabited. And the final vision of Scripture in Revelation is the full restoration of that reality: the dwelling place of God with humanity forever.

The Bible begins with presence. It ends with presence. And everything in between is the story of God bringing His people back into it.

And yet many believers live largely unaware of that reality. Many live busy, distracted, spiritually exhausted lives—longing for something deeper but unsure how to find it. Many know about God. Far fewer cultivate life with Him.

That is not condemnation. It is observation.

The modern world has discipled us into hurry, distraction, and noise. We are constantly connected, yet internally fragmented. We consume more information than ever before, yet many remain spiritually undernourished.

We have access to endless content. But access is not intimacy. Information is not communion. Activity is not presence. And because of that, many believers settle for religious routine when relational nearness is available. This book is my attempt to help.

Not because I have mastered this life or figured it all out—I have not. But because I have walked enough roads with God to know His faithfulness. And I have learned that the best life you can live is the life lived near Him.

In these pages, you will find stories from my own life. Not because my story is unique, but because it is honest. I use my own story for two reasons.

First, I am more comfortable exposing my own weaknesses than someone else's. Second, I know these stories are true. I have lived them. And in them, I have witnessed firsthand the faithfulness of God.

You will find stories of hardship, suffering, waiting, healing, obedience, family struggle, mission work, and moments of deep uncertainty. You will also find moments of joy, breakthrough, wonder, and divine interruption. Not because the Christian life is easy. But because it is real. And it is often in the real places where God makes Himself known most clearly.

This book is built around one central conviction:

**We were made to live as people of His presence.**

Not occasional visitors. Not distant observers. People. Women and men who live consciously aware of God's nearness. People shaped by His voice. Formed by His Spirit. Anchored by His peace. And sent into the world carrying His light.

The first three chapters explore encounter—how God meets us in unexpected places, interrupts our mess, and calls us into deeper dependence on His presence.

The next three chapters explore formation—how His presence produces peace, shapes our homes, and forms the character of Christ in us through the work of the Holy Spirit.

The final two chapters explore mission and sustained devotion—how a life shaped by God's presence becomes light in the world and how we intentionally cultivate a life of continual awareness, devotion, and obedience.

This is not a book about spiritual perfection. It is a book about spiritual pursuit. It is an invitation. To slow down. To pay attention. To draw near. To stop settling for religious routine when relational nearness is available.

My prayer is simple: That somewhere in these pages you would become more aware of God's nearness. That your hunger for Him would deepen. That your devotion would grow. That your faith would strengthen. And that your life would increasingly reflect the presence of the God who has always been near. Because the greatest gift God gives us is not merely what He does for us.

It is Himself.

And the best life you can live is the life lived in His presence.

Welcome to the journey.

# Part I

# Encounter

# Chapter 1
# God in the Middle

*God often meets us in the middle places of life—especially the places we did not choose.*

Many imagine God is easiest to find in ideal conditions—quiet mornings, ordered lives, healthy relationships, stable finances, and predictable futures. But Scripture tells a different story.

More often than not, God meets people in disruption—when plans collapse, relationships fracture, and the future becomes uncertain. I have learned personally that in disaster and disappointment, God often meets desperation.

Jacob, the patriarch who would father the nation of Israel, knew disruption well. Genesis 28 opens with Jacob in crisis—running for his life because of his own choices. He had participated in a scheme, a deception that was supposed to secure his future, but instead it sent him on a trajectory of uncertainty and shame.

Jacob and his brother Esau were twins, but opposites in nearly every way. Esau was rugged, outdoors-oriented, instinctive. Jacob was calculating, strategic, and often manipulative. Their relationship was marked by rivalry from the beginning. Competition defined them. Conflict shaped them. Jacob, true to his nature, maneuvered his way into securing what belonged to his brother. First, the birthright. Then, the blessing. What began as family dysfunction escalated into betrayal. Esau's anger became murderous. Jacob ran. And this is where the story becomes deeply human.

Jacob was not running because of persecution. He was running because of his own decisions. His crisis was self-inflicted. That matters. Because many of us know what it is like to suffer from our own choices. Not all wilderness is imposed on us. Some wilderness we create. Jacob fled with nothing but fear and uncertainty. No home. No protection. No guarantee of tomorrow.

**Personal Wilderness**

I know what it feels like when life begins to unravel. For me, it began in the summer of 2013. At first, it seemed like isolated problems. My back went out. Not minor pain—total collapse. For two weeks I crawled around the house because I could not walk. Then came severe stomach pain. Not discomfort. Agony.

Living in Nepal at the time, I began a long process of medical investigation. Doctors discovered three separate bacterial infections in my gut, one of them E. coli. They performed an endoscopy.
Nothing.

A colonoscopy.
Nothing.

So they sent me to Bangkok. More procedures. More tests. Still nothing. Then I was sent back to the United States to see an infectious disease specialist.
Again, nothing.

No answers.

Only symptoms, pain, and confusion. And if suffering is difficult, suffering without explanation is often worse. Pain with no diagnosis creates its own kind of fear.

What is happening to me?

Why can no one figure this out?

Will I ever recover?

At the time, I was actively serving in ministry, and my inability to function physically created something deeper than frustration. It created shame. I felt like I was failing. Failing my calling. Failing my family. Failing my responsibilities. The weakness became spiritual and emotional, not just physical.

I began meeting with a therapist, trying to navigate the emotional fallout of what my body could no longer do. And through one of those conversations, he encouraged me to see a brain surgeon he knew.

At that point, it felt random. A last-ditch effort. One more opinion. One more dead end. But that recommendation changed everything. A CT scan of my head revealed a cyst in my brain. At first, doctors minimized it. "It's probably nothing." But at a follow-up appointment, the tone changed. It was more serious than they had initially communicated.

Through different connections I met a Christian brain surgeon who agreed to take my case. After surgery, he told me that the cyst was the size of a large egg. It had been under such intense pressure from my brain that when he punctured it to drain the fluid, it erupted like a geyser. He literally had to jump back to avoid being struck.

It was far worse than anyone realized. And in that moment, I realized something profound: What felt like meaningless suffering had been guiding me toward hidden danger. What I thought was interruption was actually mercy. Even the painful road had purpose. That does not mean the journey was easy. It wasn't.

Recovery was grueling. Harder than expected. And even now, my body carries reminders of that season. Things as simple as swinging on a swing or riding a roller coaster trigger intense nausea. My body remembers. And so does my soul. But perhaps the hardest part was not the surgery. It was the humiliation along the way.

In Nepal, medical treatment often lacked dignity and compassion. In Bangkok, I was questioned about AIDS because we operated an AIDS hospice. Though there had been no sexual misconduct, no moral failure, and no reason to suspect such things beyond occupational exposure, I was treated with suspicion and contempt. Like I was unclean. Like I was less than human.

Suffering often carries humiliation. Job knew that. Jesus knew that. And many of us do too.

Even after returning to the States, we sought healing in every place we knew. At one point, I went to the healing rooms at Bethel Church in Redding. God healed others.

Not me.

Not then.

And that may be one of the hardest spiritual realities to accept: What do you do when God heals others but not you? What do you do when breakthrough happens beside you but not for you?

**Wilderness Encounter**

Jacob's wilderness looked different than mine, but the questions were the same. Questions asked in the dark. Questions asked in wilderness. Questions asked with stones for pillows. And it was there—amid uncertainty, pain, humiliation, and delay—that I learned something vital: God is not only present in miracles. He is present in mystery.

In the middle of his chaos, Jacob had a vision of heaven, angels ascending and descending from an out-of-this-world ladder. He had stumbled into an encounter with God. Jacob discovered God on the run. I discovered Him in the unraveling. In his surprise, he confessed his revelation, "This is surely the house of God, and I did not know it!"

And often, the middle places we would never choose become the places where God reveals Himself most clearly. That is where Jacob found Him. Not in strength, when he was at his best. Not in success, when every resource still seemed within reach. Not in peace when he had his life all planned out and dreaming of wealth and prosperity. But on the run.

And somewhere along the journey, exhausted and vulnerable, he stopped for the night. Scripture says he took a stone for his pillow. A stone. No comfort. No shelter. No security. Just earth beneath him and stars above him. And it was there—on the ground, in the middle of consequence, uncertainty, and exhaustion—that God came near. Jacob dreamed. A ladder stretched from earth to heaven.

Angels ascending and descending. And above it stood the Lord. This is one of the great revelations of Scripture: God is not absent in the hidden places. He is present there. Jacob was not in church. Not at an altar. Not in a sacred gathering. He was on the side of the road.

Alone.

Running.

Broken.

And God came.

This changes how we understand encounter. Many people assume God only shows up in spiritual environments. Sunday worship. Prayer meetings. Sacred spaces. But Jacob teaches us that God often invades ordinary, painful, unplanned places. Hospital rooms. Waiting rooms. Operating rooms. Funeral homes. Lonely apartments. Long roads. Unexpected places.

I discovered this before brain surgery. There is something about facing the possibility of loss that strips away illusion. You stop negotiating with superficial things. Presence becomes everything. In those moments, I learned that peace is not confidence in an outcome. Peace is confidence in God. And when His presence becomes real, fear loses its dominance.

Jacob awoke and said: “Surely the Lord is in this place, and I did not know it” (Genesis 28:16).

That statement may be one of the most honest spiritual realizations in all of Scripture. God was already there. Jacob simply became aware. This is often how divine encounter works. God’s presence precedes our awareness of it. He is already present in the crisis. Already present in the pain. Already present in the confusion. We awaken to what was already true. Jacob named that place Bethel—House of God. Think about that. He turned a place of crisis into a place of remembrance. What looked like interruption became revelation.

What looked like displacement became destiny. That is what the presence of God does. It transforms geography into theology. A roadside becomes a sanctuary. A stone becomes an altar. A fugitive becomes a patriarch. And Jacob changed.

**Encounter Must Mature**

Jacob's encounter at Bethel changed something in him, but it did not complete him. That is important. One encounter with God can redirect your life, but transformation is often a process. Bethel was the beginning. Not the finish.

Years later, Jacob would find himself in another defining moment in Genesis 32. This time, he was not running from Esau. He was returning to him. And fear had returned with him. The same brother he had betrayed years earlier was now approaching with four hundred men. Jacob feared the worst. The wounds of the past had not fully disappeared. Old decisions still cast long shadows.

And in the night, Jacob wrestled.

Not with Esau.

With God.

Or at least with a mysterious divine messenger representing God's confrontation with Jacob's soul. This matters because Bethel gave Jacob revelation. Peniel gave Jacob transformation. At Bethel, Jacob saw God. At Peniel, God touched Jacob. At Bethel, Jacob received promise. At Peniel,

Jacob received a wound. And sometimes the deepest work of God in our lives is not through what He shows us, but through what He changes in us. Jacob wrestled all night. And at daybreak, the Lord touched his hip and dislocated it.

Then something remarkable happened. Jacob refused to let go. “I will not let you go unless you bless me.” That is the language of desperation. Not casual spirituality. Not convenience. Dependence. And then God asked Jacob his name. That seems strange. God knew his name. But Jacob needed to say it. Jacob.

The deceiver.

The manipulator.

The grabber.

Names mattered. Identity mattered. And then God renamed him: Israel. One who wrestles with God. Jacob left that encounter limping. Changed. Marked. Different. That is often how encounter works. We want God to remove pain. Sometimes He transforms us through it. We want instant healing. Sometimes He gives deeper holiness. We want relief. He often gives transformation.

I understand that now in ways I could not understand in 2013. When I look back at that season—pain, surgery, uncertainty, humiliation—I see that God was doing more than preserving my life.

He was reshaping it. Weakness was teaching dependence. Pain was exposing pride. Limitations were confronting self-reliance. I entered that season wanting answers. I came out needing God. And sometimes that is the greater miracle. Not that circumstances changed. But that we changed. Jacob walked away from Bethel awakened. Jacob walked away from Peniel transformed. That is the journey of presence. First awakening. Then transformation.

**Encountering the Gospel Ladder**

That encounter redirected his life. He went from striving to surrendering. From manipulating to depending. From running to returning. Presence changes people. This is the heart of the gospel. Jesus does not merely improve lives. He interrupts them. He meets us in our mess. He is not surprised by our confusion. He's simply waiting for us to realize that He is already there in the middle of our mess. Jesus explicitly references Himself as the fulfillment of Jacob's ladder (John 1:51). He is the connection point between heaven and earth. This is huge. Jacob saw access. Jesus became access. He is the access point in whatever or wherever we find ourselves.

Paul writes: "All have sinned and fall short of the glory of God" (Romans 3:23). In many ways, the human condition is Jacob's condition. Running from our problems. Broken from our sinful condition. Separated from the things that we need. But the gospel declares that God comes near.

And through Christ, access is restored. "The wages of sin is death, but the free gift of God is eternal life in Christ Jesus our Lord" (Romans 6:23). And: "Everyone who calls on the name of the Lord will be saved" (Romans 10:13). God still meets people in middle places. In surgery. In suffering. In crisis. In repentance. In surrender.

And often, the places we would never choose become the places we encounter Him most deeply. His presence becomes the sanctuary. Contact with His presence becomes the deepest place of contentment. Jacob's ladder was more than a dream. It was a sign. A picture of access between heaven and earth. And in Christ, that access becomes personal. God does not merely send a ladder. He comes Himself.

The God Jacob encountered in mystery would later be revealed fully in Jesus. The invitation is not to wait for cleaner circumstances or calmer conditions. The invitation is to awaken now—to recognize what Jacob discovered: God is here—and His presence changes everything. But encounter is only the beginning.

Jacob discovered that God was nearer than he realized. But divine encounter is never the end of the story. God does not reveal Himself merely to interrupt our lives, but to transform them.

## Chapter 1 Reflection Guide

### Reflect

1. Where in your life do you currently feel "in the middle"—between what was and what will be?

2. Have you ever experienced a season where suffering or uncertainty became a place of deeper encounter with God? What did He reveal to you there?

3. Like Jacob, are there consequences from your own choices that have created a difficult season? How might God still meet you there?

4. What "unexpected places" in your life might God be using right now to reveal His presence?

5. When you face uncertainty, what do you instinctively trust first—your control, your plans, or God's presence?

---

### Respond

This week, identify one "middle place" in your life—a situation that feels unresolved, painful, or uncertain.

Instead of asking first, **"How do I get out of this?"**

Ask:

**"God, how do You want to meet me here?"**

Write down what that place is and spend ten uninterrupted minutes inviting God into it in prayer.

Do not rush. Do not fix. Just become aware.

---

**Pray**

Lord,

thank You that You are not absent in the middle places of my life.

Thank You that You meet me in uncertainty, pain, and transition.

Forgive me for the times I have looked for escape before I looked for You.

Open my eyes to recognize Your presence in the places I least expect it.

Like Jacob, awaken me to the reality that You are nearer than I realize.

Help me trust You in the middle and surrender what I cannot control.

Meet me here, Lord.

And let this place of struggle become a place of encounter.

In Jesus' name, amen.

# Chapter 2
# The Jesus Effect

*Jesus meets us in our brokenness not to condemn us, but to heal what only His living water can satisfy.*

*The same grace that finds us in our mess transforms us into living testimony.*

Some encounters change the trajectory of your life. A conversation. A moment. A confrontation. A revelation. A single encounter with the right person at the right moment can alter everything. The Jesus effect is the transforming influence of Christ over the life of the one who encounters Him. Not information. Not religion. Encounter. There is a difference.

She came at noon because noon was safer. Fewer eyes. Fewer whispers. Fewer questions. Jesus was traveling from Judea to Galilee, and John tells us something unusual: "He had to pass through Samaria" (John 4:4). That statement carries more than geography. It carries mission.

Information can educate you. Religion can organize you. But encounter transforms you. That is what happened to a woman at a well. And that is still what happens today. Jacob found God unexpectedly. The Samaritan woman was found intentionally.

Most Jews avoided Samaria. The hostility between Jews and Samaritans ran deep. The divide was ethnic, theological, and historical. Centuries of conflict had built walls between them. Faith had become tribal. Worship had become territorial. Resentment had become inherited.

A typical Jewish traveler would take the longer route just to avoid Samaritan territory altogether. But Jesus went through it. Because there was someone there. A woman. Unnamed. Uncelebrated. Unwanted. But seen by God. That matters.

The Bible never gives her name. But Jesus knew it. Jesus knew her story. Jesus knew her pain. Jesus knew her shame. And He went there for her. That is one of the most beautiful realities of the gospel: God knows exactly where to find us.

## Divine Interruptions

When Jesus arrived at Jacob's well, it was noon. The hottest part of the day. Not the normal time for drawing water. Women typically came in the morning or evening, when the heat was bearable and community was present. But this woman came alone. That detail matters. Loneliness often tells a story.

People who live under shame often adjust their schedules to avoid exposure. She came when no one else would be there. No conversations. No stares. No whispers. No reminders.

But Jesus was there. Waiting. Tired from the journey. Human. Present. Accessible. And He asked her for water.

The request itself was shocking. A Jewish man speaking to a Samaritan woman in public violated social expectations. Her response reveals her surprise: "How is it that you, a Jew, ask for a drink from me, a woman of Samaria?" (John 4:9).

She likely assumed what many wounded people assume: He must want something. He must think He is better than me. This can't be sincere. Wounded people often struggle to trust love. But Jesus was not there to take. He was there to give.

**Living Water**

Jesus quickly moved the conversation from natural thirst to spiritual thirst. "If you knew the gift of God..." (John 4:10). He offered her living water. Water that satisfies at the deepest level.

Jesus exposed something universal: We all thirst. Not physically alone. Spiritually. Emotionally. Existentially. And much of life is spent trying to satisfy that thirst. We look for satisfaction in relationships, success, pleasure, recognition, and distraction.

But Jesus says: You can keep returning to the same wells and remain thirsty. That is the tragedy of human striving. We return to broken wells. Over and over. Expecting satisfaction. Finding depletion. Augustine of Hippo wrote in *Confessions*, "You have made us for Yourself, and our hearts are restless until they rest in you."[1] This woman knew that restless cycle. And Jesus knew that of her too.

### The Wells We Keep Returning To

The tragedy of human life is not merely that we thirst. It is where we keep going to satisfy that thirst.

Jesus offered the woman living water because He knew something about the human soul: it keeps searching for permanence in temporary things. We all build wells. Some are obvious. Some are respectable. Some are hidden beneath ambition, productivity, and achievement. But every person has places they return to hoping to find life.

For some, it is relationships. We convince ourselves that if the right person would love us, we would finally feel whole. For others, it is success. If I can achieve enough, earn enough, build enough, then maybe I will feel secure. For others, it is distraction. Entertainment. Social media. Busyness. Noise.

Anything to avoid thirst. The problem is not that these things are always sinful. The problem is that they make terrible saviors. They cannot hold the weight of what we ask them to carry.

This woman had built wells through relationships. Five husbands. A current relationship outside covenant. Jesus

---

[1] Augustine of Hippo, *Confessions*, Book I, Chapter 1.

was not merely counting her failures. He was exposing a pattern. A cycle. A thirst. And if we are honest, many of us know that cycle.

Returning.

Trying.

Reaching.

Hoping.

Still thirsty. That is why Jesus' invitation is so powerful. He does not merely offer improvement. He offers replacement. Not another well. A new source. Living water. Water that does not merely refresh, but renew. Water that does not merely sustain, but satisfies. And this is the invitation of Christ to every restless heart: stop drinking from broken wells.

Come to the source. That is easier said than done. Because often, the wells we drink from are familiar. And familiar dysfunction can feel safer than unfamiliar healing. But Jesus calls us beyond familiarity. Into freedom.

### He Meets Us in the Mess

Jesus did not avoid her mess. He entered it. "Go call your husband." Simple words. But deeply exposing. Her answer was partial truth. "I have no husband." And Jesus lovingly uncovered the deeper truth. Five husbands. And the current relationship outside covenant.

Jesus knew everything. And stayed. This is grace. Not approval of sin. But refusal to abandon sinners. Jesus never minimized her brokenness. But He did not weaponize it either. He revealed it to heal it.

This is how grace works.

God confronts what He intends to heal. Many people assume Jesus only comes when life is cleaned up. But this story teaches the opposite: Jesus comes in the mess. In addiction. In broken relationships. In regret. In shame. In cycles. In failure.

He comes there. Because that is where we are. And He loves us enough not to leave us there.

### The Great Human Fear

One of humanity's deepest fears is this: If people knew everything about me, they would reject me. But Jesus knows everything. And still moves toward us.

This is the scandal of grace. Not that God tolerates sinners. That He pursues them. He knows every thought. Every compromise. Every hidden wound. Every repeated failure. And still says: Come.

That is what makes grace transformational. Not because it ignores truth. But because it applies love to truth.

**When Jesus Names the Wound**

Jesus did not expose her to shame her. He exposed her to heal her. That distinction matters. Conviction and condemnation are not the same thing. Condemnation pushes you away. Conviction pulls you closer. Condemnation says: Hide. Conviction says: Come into the light.

That is why Jesus named her story. Not to humiliate her. To liberate her. Healing often begins where honesty begins. That is one of the reasons many people avoid deep prayer. Because deep prayer invites deep honesty.

And honesty is costly. It means naming wounds. Naming fears. Naming patterns. Naming sins. Naming grief. But what remains unnamed often remains unhealed. Jesus names what we avoid because He intends to restore what has been broken.

I have seen this in my own life.

There have been seasons where the Holy Spirit confronted places in me I did not want to face—fear, pride, self-reliance, insecurity. Not because God wanted to shame me. Because He loved me enough to heal me. God confronts what He intends to transform. And often, the places we most want to protect are the places He most wants to heal.

**Excuses and Evasion**

When the conversation became personal, the woman changed the subject. Religion. Location. Tradition. Debate.

This is human instinct. When God touches the wound, we often change the subject.

We intellectualize. Deflect. Argue. Rationalize. Jesus did not follow her into distraction. He stayed on the deeper issue. That is important. Jesus will not validate our excuses. He loves us too much. He does not accommodate avoidance. He invites surrender.

That can feel confrontational. But it is mercy.

## Worship in Spirit and Truth

Jesus redirected the conversation from place to posture. Not this mountain. Not Jerusalem. But spirit and truth. True worship is not geographical. It is relational. The Father seeks worshipers. That is astonishing.

God seeks people. Not performance. Not perfection. People.

And He seeks those willing to come honestly. Truthfully. Humbly. This woman had built her life around hiding. Jesus invited her into worship. Because worship heals what hiding never can.

## Revelation Belongs to the Humble

Then came the great moment. The woman spoke of Messiah. And Jesus plainly revealed Himself. “I who speak to you am he.”

This is one of the clearest self-revelations of Jesus in the Gospel of John. And who receives it? Not a religious leader. Not a Pharisee. Not a scholar. A broken woman at a well. Why? Because humility opens doors pride cannot. Jesus reveals Himself to those who come honestly. Not impressively. Honestly.

**The Jesus Effect**

The story does not end at the well. She leaves changed. She leaves her water jar. That detail is symbolic. The thing she came for became irrelevant because she found what she actually needed. Then she ran into town.

The woman who avoided people became the woman who pursued them. Encountering Jesus changed her. Shame became testimony. What she Isolated from became her mission field.

This is the Jesus effect.

One encounter changes everything. Not because life becomes perfect. But because identity changes. Purpose changes. Desire changes. Direction changes. The Jesus effect is still happening. Not just in faraway places. Not just on mission fields. Not just in revival meetings.

Right here. Right now.

In homes. In churches. In ordinary lives. Jesus still meets people in their mess. I have seen this personally. Not only in my own life, but in the strange and surprising ways Jesus pursues people.

### From Hiding to Witness

One of the most remarkable parts of this story is what happens next. The woman leaves her water jar. John includes that detail intentionally (John 4:28). The jar mattered. It was why she came. It was her purpose for the day.

Her practical need.

And yet after encountering Jesus, she left it behind. Because when you find living water, old priorities begin to shift. What once felt urgent becomes secondary. What once defined your day loses its grip. And she ran into the city. The same city she had likely been avoiding. The same people she had structured her life around avoiding.

Now she runs toward them.

That is transformation. Encounter changed her relationship with people because encounter changed her relationship with herself. Shame had lost its power. Grace had changed her posture. And her testimony was remarkably simple: “Come and see a man who told me all that I ever did.”

Not: Come hear my theology.

Not: Come hear my argument.

Not: Come hear my polished presentation.

Just: Come and see.

That is the power of testimony. You do not have to know everything to tell what Jesus has done for you. Evangelism often begins there. Not with expertise. With encounter. Not with perfection. With honesty.

Your story can become a bridge. Your healing can become a witness. Your encounter can become someone else's invitation. And that is exactly what happened. Because of one woman's testimony, many in that Samaritan town came to believe. One encounter changed one woman. And one changed woman affected a city.

That is still how the kingdom works. Not through polished platforms alone. But through transformed people.

## An Encounter of Correction

When I was twenty-two years old, I had one of the clearest moments of divine correction in my life. As a child, I had a vision of Jesus telling me I would one day be a missionary.

At nine, I believed it. But at twenty-two, I questioned it. By then, life had changed. I had graduated from college and was serving as a youth pastor under my father. Ministry was going well. Teenagers were being saved. The youth ministry was growing. There was momentum, fruit, and purpose. And quietly, I began rethinking my future.

Before one midweek youth service, I remember telling the Lord plainly that I must have misunderstood Him as a child.

A nine-year-old could not possibly hear from God clearly enough to determine the trajectory of an entire life. At least that's what I thought.

The service went well. Nothing too dramatic happened. The next morning was my day off. I was trying to sleep in when our landline phone began ringing. And ringing. And ringing. More than twenty-five times. Old landlines were not supposed to ring like that. Finally, out of frustration, I answered. It was a telemarketer selling vacation timeshares.

I tried to be polite and explained that I was far too poor for timeshares—I was a youth pastor. She paused and asked:

"Are you a Christian?"

I said yes.

Then she told me she was a Muslim immigrant from Iran. What followed was one of the strangest and most sacred conversations of my life. We began talking about the differences between Christianity and Islam. At one point I said:

"In Christianity, there is forgiveness for sins."

And she replied:

"In Islam, there is no assurance of forgiveness."

That sentence hung in the air. So I asked her: "Would you like to be forgiven of your sins?" And she said yes. Right there, over the phone, I led her in a simple prayer of repentance and faith in Jesus. I encouraged her to find a church and get a Bible.

And when the call ended, the Holy Spirit immediately confronted me. He brought back to my mind the conversation I had with Him the night before. "You told Me you misunderstood My call. And yet here was a Muslim woman—someone you could have never reached in Iran—calling you directly in your room."

God had brought the mission field to me.

And the Holy Spirit impressed something deeply into my heart: "Do not tell Me what a nine-year-old can hear. Do not tell Me whom I have called. Do not tell Me what doors I can open."

He had called me. And in due time, He opened those doors. That moment taught me something essential: Jesus still pursues people. Across boundaries. Across distance. Across religious systems. Across our doubts. And often, He interrupts our ordinary lives to remind us that His mission is still moving.

That is the Jesus effect.

He changes people. And sometimes, He changes us while changing someone else. He still offers living water, exposes shame, reveals Himself, and transforms lives.

The question is not whether Jesus is willing to meet you. The question is whether you are willing to come honestly. Because one encounter with Him can change everything.

Jesus is willing to cross boundaries we are unwilling to cross.

Encounter is not the end of the Christian life. It is the beginning. Transformation must mature into devotion. The God who finds us also invites us to remain near Him.

## Chapter 2 Reflection Guide

### Reflect

1. What "wells" do you find yourself returning to for satisfaction, comfort, or identity apart from God (success, approval, relationships, distraction, achievement, comfort)?

2. Are there areas of your life where shame has caused you to isolate yourself from others—or from God?

3. Like the woman at the well, are there painful parts of your story you would rather avoid than surrender to Jesus?

4. What does it mean to you that Jesus already knows everything about you and still moves toward you in love?

5. Where in your life do you sense Jesus inviting you to deeper honesty?

---

**Respond**

Identify one “well” in your life that you have been drawing from for satisfaction that is not ultimately giving life.

Name it honestly.

Write it down.

Then ask yourself:

**What am I hoping this gives me that only Jesus can provide?**

This week, intentionally replace one return to that false well with time in God’s presence—through prayer, worship, or Scripture.

Choose living water over empty wells.

---

**Pray**

Jesus,

thank You for meeting me where I am, not where I pretend to be.

Thank You for seeing my whole story and loving me completely.

Forgive me for returning to wells that cannot satisfy my soul.

Forgive me for looking for life in places that leave me empty.
Give me courage to be honest with You and honest with myself.
Heal the places in me marked by shame, regret, and brokenness.
Fill me with Your living water and teach me to thirst for You above all else.
Change me through Your presence, and make my life a testimony of Your grace.
In Jesus' name, amen.

# Chapter 3
# If Your Presence Does Not Go with Us

*The Christian life is not sustained by occasional visitations from God, but by abiding in His presence.*

*What we desire most reveals whether we want God for His gifts or God for Himself.*

Encounter may begin the journey, but devotion sustains it. Some encounters with God come in moments of power; others come in moments of pain.

I learned this in Nepal.

In Nepal, the realities of faith were rarely theoretical. A Hindu activist in our area had planted a bomb in a local church—only ten houses from where my family and I were living. The explosion shook our neighborhood so violently that every picture hanging on the walls of our rented home trembled. It was a vivid reminder that the kingdom of darkness resists the kingdom of God.

After his arrest, believers gathered to pray for him. I remember praying intensely—not for judgment, but for salvation. Later we learned that someone in prison had led him to Christ, and for a brief moment he professed faith in Jesus. But over time, he recanted that confession and returned to his former beliefs and activism against Christianity.

Ministry teaches you that spiritual conflict is rarely simple. Not every confession endures. Not every seed immediately takes root. But the call of the church remains the same: pray, intercede, love enemies, and trust God with outcomes.

I left that prayer meeting hopeful. But spiritual victory does not always mean immediate ease. When I returned home, the atmosphere in our house felt different.

My wife, Bethany, met me at the door and told me our two-and-a-half-year-old son had not eaten. At first, it seemed small. Children skip meals. But he was not a child who skipped meals. He had always had a healthy appetite. The next day, he still would not eat.

Then another day.

Then another.

When offered food, he would politely smile and say, "No thanks," before running off to play. At first it was strange. Then concerning. Then terrifying.

After ten days, we took him to the doctor. We searched for every possible explanation. Interventions were tried.

Nothing changed. He still would not eat. Around that same time, I was scheduled to leave for a ministry trek deep into the mountains. I wrestled with whether I should go. I remember talking with Bethany about it. I told her plainly: "I do not want to leave and have our son die while I'm gone." She looked at me and told me to go. And then she said something I have never forgotten: "If he dies while you're gone, I will not hold it against you."

It was one of the hardest decisions I have ever made.

The journey itself felt like resistance. We drove for hours through difficult terrain to pick up our interpreter. Along the way, we had two flat tires. The next day we drove until the road ended. Then, before sunrise the next morning, we began trekking.

We started at four in the morning and walked all day until nearly eight o'clock that night. Our guide told us we had covered at least eighty kilometers that day. It was exhausting.

That week we ministered in remote villages—preaching, teaching, baptizing, encouraging believers. But every moment I carried a private fear: What if my son dies while I am away? On the final night before returning home, I called Bethany.

Her voice was heavy.

She told me our son still had not eaten solid food. Then she said something that hit me like a blow: "I gave him a bath tonight. I could count every rib." Bethany is a registered nurse. She has cared for critically ill patients. She does not exaggerate. She thought our son was dying. I tried to sound brave on the phone. I told her everything would be okay. But when I hung up, I knew I did not believe my own words.

That night, I had one of the most honest conversations with God I have ever had.

I bargained.

I pleaded.

I made promises. “God, I’ll do anything if You heal my son.” And then, in the silence, I sensed the Holy Spirit confront me with a question I did not want to hear:

**What if I take him?**

What would you do? Would you leave Me? Would you stop serving Me? Would you walk away? It was not cruelty. It was revelation. God was exposing the depth of my trust.

And through tears, my answer came: “I would be devastated. I would be broken. But where else could I go? You have the words of life. I would grieve—but I would still serve You.”

That was the moment everything changed.

Not because the miracle came immediately. But because His presence came. When I finally returned, we made our way to Bangkok to seek better medical care. But before our son ever saw a doctor—before medicine, before treatment—he began eating again.

Solid food.

Just like that.

We received it as mercy. As miracle. As God's intervention. The full recovery took nearly a year. But in that moment, God answered. Looking back, I learned something in that wilderness: God's greatest gift in crisis is not always immediate deliverance. Sometimes His greatest gift is Himself.

Moses understood this when he prayed: "If your presence will not go with me, do not bring us up from here" (Exodus 33:15). Moses knew what suffering teaches every believer eventually: If God's presence is with you, even the wilderness can sustain you.

Many seek God for what He gives—healing, provision, breakthrough, direction. These are gifts, and gifts are good. But gifts are never the goal. God Himself is the goal.

But if His presence is absent, even the Promised Land is empty. That is what it means to become a person of His presence. There are trials that expose what you actually believe about God. Not in theory. Not in theology. But in the midnight hours when fear sits at the end of the bed and refuses to leave.

Many modern believers still pursue promised lands—success, stability, influence, security—without asking first whether God's presence is leading them there. Modern promised lands often look like the pursuit of success, security, influence, recognition or ministry momentum.

In seasons like that, you discover something essential: sometimes the greatest miracle is not immediate deliverance, but the sustaining presence of God in the middle of uncertainty.

That is what Moses understood.

There are moments in life when progress can become a substitute for presence. We move forward. We build. We accomplish. We accumulate. We achieve. Yet beneath the momentum lies a deeper question: Is God with us?

It is possible to attend church, sing songs, hear sermons, and maintain spiritual habits while remaining largely disconnected from the living presence of God. Religious activity, while valuable, can never replace divine communion. Programs can organize people, but only the presence of God can transform them.

Moses realized this.

In Exodus 33, Israel stood on the edge of promise. The land of inheritance was before them. The covenant promise was within reach. Yet something had been fractured. Israel had sinned grievously through the golden calf, and the relational tension between divine holiness and human rebellion was exposed.

God promised movement.

Moses wanted presence.

The distinction matters.

The Lord said to Moses, “My presence will go with you, and I will give you rest” (Exod. 33:14). Moses responded with one of the most important prayers in Scripture: “If your presence will not go with me, do not bring us up from here” (Exod. 33:15).

Moses understood what many modern believers forget: the promise without the presence is empty.

The land meant nothing if God was absent.

Better wilderness with God than abundance without Him. Wilderness has a way of clarifying what matters most. That prayer reveals a profound spiritual priority. Moses valued communion over conquest, relationship over reward, presence over progress. The defining mark of God’s people is not merely that they believe in God, but desire Him.

## More Than Theology

In Scripture, the presence of God is not merely an abstract doctrine. It is experiential, relational, and transformative. The psalmist writes, “In your presence there is fullness of joy” (Psalms 16:11). Peter preached that “times of refreshing” come from the presence of the Lord (Acts 3:19). These texts reveal something vital: God’s presence is not merely conceptual. It is experiential.

New Testament theology has always insisted upon this reality. God is not merely known cognitively but encountered personally through the ministry of the Holy Spirit. The Spirit mediates the active, living presence of God among His people.

There is an important distinction here. God's **omnipresence** means He is everywhere. God's **manifest presence** means He makes Himself known. This distinction shapes the Christian life. A person can affirm God's omnipresence and still neglect His manifest presence.

It is the difference between reading letters from someone you love and sitting in the room with them. One is information. The other is communion. The Christian life was never designed to stop at information. It was designed for presence.

## Omnipresence Is Not the Same as Communion

One of the easiest mistakes in spiritual life is assuming that because God is everywhere, we are automatically walking with Him.

That is not the same thing.

God's omnipresence means there is nowhere He is absent. Psalm 139 tells us there is no place we can go where God is not already present. If we ascend to heaven, He is there. If we descend into the depths, He is there.

That is the theological reality of omnipresence.

But omnipresence is not the same as communion. A husband may be physically in the room with his wife and yet emotionally distant. Proximity does not guarantee intimacy.

The same is true spiritually.

Many believers affirm God's omnipresence while living with little awareness of His nearness. God is present. But they are inattentive. That is often the issue. Not divine absence. Human distraction. This is why the spiritual life requires intentionality.

Awareness.

Attention.

Participation.

The question is not whether God is near. The question is whether we are awake. Jacob said, "Surely the Lord is in this place, and I did not know it." God was there before Jacob noticed. Awareness changed everything. And that remains true. Much of spiritual maturity is growing in awareness of what has already been made available.

### The Difference Between Visitation and Abiding

There is a difference between visitation and abiding. Throughout the Old Testament, God's presence often came in moments.

Burning bushes.

Cloud by day.

Fire by night.

Temple glory.

Prophetic moments.

These were visitations—real, powerful, holy. But temporary. Under the new covenant, Jesus introduces something deeper. Abiding. In John 15, Jesus repeatedly says, "Abide in me."

Remain.

Stay.

Live connected.

The Christian life is not merely built on spiritual moments. It is built on spiritual continuity. This is where many believers struggle. They live from conference to conference. Service to service. Altar moment to altar moment. Always needing another spiritual high.

But God did not design us to live on occasional visitations. He designed us for abiding. For rootedness. For sustained communion. The goal is not merely to experience God in moments. It is to walk with Him daily.

This changes how we understand prayer. Prayer is not merely emergency response. It is abiding. Worship is not merely singing. It is abiding. Scripture is not merely study. It is abiding. Obedience is not merely discipline. It is abiding.

And abiding produces stability.

Deep roots. Lasting fruit. This is why Jesus says that apart from Him, we can do nothing. Disconnected spirituality eventually dries up. Connected spirituality bears fruit.

### Humanity Was Created for Presence

The story begins in the garden. In Genesis 3:8, God walked with Adam and Eve in the cool of the day. Before sin, humanity's natural environment was divine fellowship. The original design of humanity was not mere moral obedience but relational nearness. Presence was home.

This reframes the fall. Sin did not simply violate divine law; it ruptured divine fellowship. Humanity was exiled from the garden, and with that exile came distance. Ever since, human beings have been restless. Searching. Longing. Reaching.

A.W. Tozer reminds us that the great tragedy of spiritual life is not wanting too much from God, but wanting too little of Him. Religion can become a pursuit of benefits rather than of the Benefactor.[2]

Much of human striving can be understood as misdirected hunger for restored presence. As a child does not ultimately want gifts apart from the giver, so the human soul cannot be satisfied with blessings apart from God Himself. The blessing is never greater than the Blesser. We were made for Him.

---

[2] A.W. Tozer, *The Pursuit of God* (Christian Publications, Inc, 1948), 6.

## Jesus Restored What Sin Lost

The gospel is, in many ways, the story of restored access. At the crucifixion of Christ, the temple veil was torn from top to bottom (Matthew 27:51). This was not incidental. It was theological declaration. The barrier had been removed.

The writer of Hebrews tells believers that through the blood of Jesus we now have confidence to enter the holy places (Hebrews 10:19–22). What was once restricted became available. Under the old covenant, one priest entered once a year. Under the new covenant, every believer has access at all times. This is the miracle of grace.

There are beautiful and sacred spaces belonging to ancient Christendom like Hagia Sophia and St. Peter's Basilica, places that carry centuries of Christian memory and devotion. They inspire awe. Yet the gospel announces something greater: God is not confined to sacred architecture. Through Christ, His presence is now accessible to every believer, in every place.

And Pentecost takes the restoration even further. In Acts 2, the presence of God no longer simply dwells in sacred space. He fills sacred people. The Spirit who once descended upon places now indwells believers. The church is not merely a gathering place for God's presence. It is a carrier of God's presence. We do not go somewhere to find Him. We carry Him into the world.

## The Marks of Presence-Shaped People

Preparing for brain surgery taught me something sobering: prayer becomes less polished when mortality becomes real. I learned then that daily communion with God is not merely spiritual discipline—it is survival. Presence steadies you before crisis arrives and in the middle when panic tries to come in and take over. Those moments of desperation, Holy Spirit comes overwhelmingly so. Peace like a river is not a simple children's song, it is a forceful reality. Thanks be to God!

What does a life shaped by divine presence look like?

### Hunger

God-centered people are marked by hunger. "As a deer pants for flowing streams, so pants my soul for you, O God" (Psalms 42:1). Spiritual hunger distinguishes living faith from dead routine. Presence cannot be replaced by habit. Routine may sustain structure, but it cannot satisfy longing. And when routine cannot satiate the needs of the soul, hunger takes over and produces desire. Desire then gives way to new habits and practices.

### Practice

Spirit-aware people cultivate daily communion. David said, "One thing have I asked of the Lord..." (Psalms 27:4). Presence is not sustained accidentally. It is cultivated intentionally. Prayer. Worship. Stillness. Scripture. Listening.

Like a device requiring regular charging, the soul requires regular communion. Weekly contact cannot sustain daily formation.

## Reflection

Presence-shaped people reflect what they behold. Paul writes that believers are transformed from glory to glory (2 Corinthians 3:18). This mirrors Moses in Exodus 34, whose face shone after communion with God. Presence leaves residue. It changes speech. Attitudes. Priorities. Relationships. People can often tell who has been with Jesus.

## What Presence Produces

Isaiah's encounter in Isaiah 6 provides a pattern. First, he saw the Lord. Then, he saw himself. Then, he was cleansed. Then, he was commissioned. This sequence remains instructive. Presence reveals God. Presence reveals us. Presence cleanses. Presence sends.

New Testament spirituality must remember this order. Power without purity becomes dangerous. Experience without transformation becomes shallow. The presence of God produces conviction, cleansing, and calling. Always.

**Presence Changes Desire**

One of the first signs of real communion with God is not merely changed behavior. It is changed desire. This is important because many Christians try to change behavior without allowing God to reshape desire.

That rarely lasts.

Presence changes what we want. What once attracted us loses power. What once felt normal begins to feel empty. What once felt satisfying begins to feel hollow. This is what happened with Moses.

After encountering God deeply, Egypt lost its appeal. The palace lost its pull. The wilderness became sacred because God was there. This is what happened with Paul. After meeting Christ, he counted everything else as loss compared to knowing Jesus (Philippians 3:8).

Presence recalibrates value.

This is one of the reasons devotion matters. Because what we behold shapes what we desire. And what we desire shapes who we become. The world is constantly discipling desire.

Advertising.

Entertainment.

Ambition.

Comparison.

But presence reorders affection. It teaches the heart what matters most. That is why spiritual hunger matters. Hunger is often the evidence of reordered desire. And where desire is reordered, devotion becomes natural. Not forced. Loved.

**The Invitation**

James writes, "Draw near to God, and he will draw near to you" (James 4:8). God is not distant. He is inviting.

I remember lying weak with dysentery in a remote village, three days from the nearest highway. In moments like that, stripped of comfort and control, you learn how near God really is. Sometimes God allows us to reach the end of ourselves so we can discover He was never far away.

The issue is not divine unwillingness. It is human availability. Will we make room? Will we prioritize presence over productivity? Will we desire God above His gifts? The church does not need better performance.

It needs deeper presence. The world does not need more polished religion. It needs people who carry the reality of God. The call remains: Become people of His presence. Presence first. Peace follows.

When God's presence becomes our priority, something begins to settle within us. Presence does not remove every storm, but it changes how we live inside them. The fruit of presence is peace.

## Chapter 3 Reflection Guide

### Reflect

1. If God gave you every blessing you wanted—but withheld His felt presence—would that be enough for you?

2. What are you currently pursuing most intensely: God Himself, or what you hope He will provide?

3. When life becomes painful or uncertain, do you move toward God or away from Him?

4. What does your daily life reveal about your hunger for God?

5. Are there areas of bargaining in your relationship with God ("If You do this, then I will…")? What would full surrender look like?

---

### Respond

Set aside fifteen uninterrupted minutes this week for one purpose:

Not to ask God for anything. Not to solve anything. Not to present requests. Just to be with Him.

Sit quietly. Worship. Read a Psalm. Listen.

Practice presence without agenda.

At the end, write one sentence:

**What did I notice about my hunger for God?**

---

**Pray**

Lord,
forgive me for the times I have wanted Your gifts more than I have wanted You.
Forgive me for pursuing blessings while neglecting Your presence.
Create in me a deeper hunger for You.
Teach me to value Your nearness above comfort, success, or answered prayers.
Like Moses, let my heart say, "If Your presence does not go with me, I do not want to go."
Remove bargaining from my faith and deepen my surrender.

Help me trust You in uncertainty and love You in every season.
Be my portion, my peace, and my greatest pursuit.
In Jesus' name, amen.

# Part II

# Formation

# Chapter 4
# Shalom Reigning

*The peace of God is not the absence of trouble, but the presence of Christ reigning in the middle of it.*

What does peace actually feel like? Have you ever been surrounded by chaos and yet felt strangely steady? When God's presence becomes our priority, peace becomes possible. Most people define peace negatively.

No conflict.

No noise.

No disruption.

No stress.

No war.

No tension.

Peace is one of the most misunderstood realities in the modern world. Most people define peace negatively: no conflict, no stress, no tension, no disruption. But biblical peace is deeper. Peace is not something we pursue directly. It is what grows where Christ reigns.

I learned something of this in Nepal during a nineteen-day shutdown with the last 48 hours a shoot-to-kill curfew. Helicopters circled overhead. Rioting broke out in the streets. The city felt suspended between fear and unpredictability. Newly married and far from home, uncertainty became part of the daily atmosphere. There were no guarantees of safety, no clear timeline, and no easy escape. Yet I discovered something unexpected: Safety and peace are not the same thing. Peace is the presence of God in the midst of danger.

Jesus never promised the absence of trouble. In fact, He promised the opposite. "In the world you will have tribulation" (John 16:33). That matters. Christianity does not offer immunity from suffering. It offers presence in suffering. And presence changes everything.

### The Biblical Meaning of Peace

The Bible's word for peace is richer than our modern understanding. In Hebrew, the word is **shalom**. In Greek, the New Testament uses **eirēnē**, building on the Hebrew concept. Shalom means peace—but also means wholeness, completeness, soundness, restoration, health, and stability. It is the idea of things being rightly ordered.

Whole.

Integrated.

As they were meant to be. Think of a completed puzzle—every piece in place, nothing missing. That is shalom. Or think of a wall rebuilt after destruction. Restored. Stable. Secure. That is shalom.

Paul writes in Romans 5:1 that being justified by faith, we have peace with God. That reconciliation becomes the foundation for what Paul later describes in Philippians 4:7 as the peace of God—a peace that guards the inner life. First reconciliation, then internal peace. Biblical peace is not simply when conflict ends. It is when wholeness is restored. That is important.

Because many people spend their lives trying to reduce conflict without ever pursuing wholeness. Quiet is not peace. Any families with small children knows that a quiet house can still be full of tension and mischief. Silence is not shalom.

Shalom is deeper. It is internal order rooted in divine presence. Jesus said: “Peace I leave with you; my peace I give to you. Not as the world gives...” (John 14:27).

His peace is different.

Why? Because His peace does not depend on circumstances. It depends on Him.

### Peace With God Comes First

Before peace can reign within us, peace must be established between us and God. This is where many people misunderstand peace. They want inner peace without first addressing spiritual reconciliation.

But Scripture always starts there. Paul writes in Romans 5:1, "Therefore, since we have been justified by faith, we have peace with God through our Lord Jesus Christ." That is foundational. Before Christ, humanity stands alienated from God—not because God withdrew from us, but because sin fractured the relationship.

Peace is not merely emotional relief. It is relational restoration. And that changes everything. Because inner turmoil often has deeper roots than circumstances. Many people feel unrest because they are carrying the weight of unresolved separation from God.

Guilt.

Shame.

Distance.

Sin creates internal instability because it was never meant to coexist with communion. But when Christ reconciles us to the Father, the war ends. Not because life becomes easy. But because our deepest conflict is resolved.

Peace with God becomes the foundation for peace within. And if that foundation is missing, all attempts at peace become temporary.

Distraction.

Escape.

Avoidance.

Management.

But not peace. True peace begins where reconciliation begins. At the cross.

## Jesus Is Our Peace

Peace is not merely something Jesus gives. It is something Jesus is. Paul writes: "He himself is our peace" (Ephesians 2:14). That is extraordinary. Jesus does not merely distribute peace. He embodies it.

Why? Because sin shattered shalom. Sin disintegrates. It fractures relationship. It disorders the soul. Paul writes: "All have sinned and fall short..." (Romans 3:23). Sin dismantled what God designed. The image remained. But fractured.

Like a puzzle overturned on the floor. Pieces everywhere. Still belonging together. But disordered. Christ came to restore what sin scattered. That is reconciliation. That is shalom.

Through the cross, Jesus rebuilt what rebellion broke. Paul says He made peace through the blood of His cross (Colossians 1:20). There is a cost to peace. Wholeness is purchased. And Christ paid.

## Let Peace Rule

Many people have peace available but not reigning. Paul writes: "Let the peace of Christ rule in your hearts" (Colossians 3:15). That word "rule" matters. It means govern. Direct. Lead. Preside. Peace must reign. But peace does not reign automatically. We decide what rules us.

Fear?

Regret?

Anxiety?

Loss?

Bitterness?

Chaos?

Or Christ?

Some people are so accustomed to chaos that peace feels uncomfortable. Stillness feels suspicious. Quiet feels dangerous. Because chaos became familiar. And familiar dysfunction can feel safer than unfamiliar peace. Others live in internal noise. Much of our anxiety comes from borrowed trouble, imagined disasters, and anxious futures.

But this is not the rule of Christ. The Prince of Peace must reign. And where He reigns, peace reigns. Not because life is easy. But because the King is present. Peace rules when we: surrender control, reject anxious imagination, practice gratitude, remain prayerful, and stay rooted in truth.

**Peace Must Be Practiced**

Peace is both a gift and a discipline. Christ gives peace. But we must learn to live inside it. This is why Paul tells believers to "let" the peace of Christ rule. That word implies participation.

Permission.

Cooperation.

Peace must be practiced.

This means slowing down enough to recognize what is ruling your inner life. For many people, anxiety rules. Not because they want it to. But because they rehearse it. Thoughts become patterns. Patterns become pathways. Pathways become internal climates. And over time, anxiety becomes the emotional default.

This is why Paul gives practical instruction in Philippians 4. Pray. Give thanks. Redirect your thoughts. Think on what is true. Peace is cultivated through repeated surrender. Repeated prayer. Repeated trust. Repeated returning.

This is one of the reasons Sabbath matters.

Sabbath interrupts the internal machinery of worry. It retrains the soul. It teaches the body that God is still sustaining the world without our constant control. Peace is not passive. It is practiced trust. And practiced trust becomes lived peace.

### Peace in the Middle

One of the most remarkable truths about Jesus is this: He calmed storms. And He walked on storms. Sometimes He removes chaos. Sometimes He walks with us in it.

Both are peace.

We often pray for the storm to stop. And on occasion it does. But other times His answer is His presence. That was true in

Nepal. It was true in illness. It was true in uncertainty. And it remains true now.

In *Renovation of the Heart*, Dallas Willard emphasizes that spiritual transformation involves the reordering of the inner life.[3] Peace is not merely external calm; it is the soul brought into alignment under God.

Peace is not the removal of what threatens you. It is the nearness of the One greater than what threatens you. This is why Jesus could sleep in storms. Because peace is not environmental. It is relational.

### Pass the Peace

Some Christian traditions practice what is called "pass the peace"—greeting one another in the name of Christ as an embodied reminder of reconciliation. This practice delivers a foundational Christian concept. Peace was never meant to stop with us. It must move through us. Paul says we are ambassadors for Christ (2 Corinthians 5:20). Ambassadors carry the message of reconciliation. The message of peace. The gospel is a peace announcement. Be reconciled to God. Be made whole. Be restored. Be brought near.

This is our ministry. Not simply greeting one another in church but to be the delivery system of peace. To bring

---

[3] Dallas Willard, *Renovation of the Heart: Putting on the Character of Christ* (NavPress, 2021), 59.

peace into homes. Marriages. Families. Neighborhoods. Churches. Communities.

The angels announced at Christ's birth: Peace on earth. And now His people continue that announcement. Not abstractly. Practically. Personally. Relationally. This holiday season, and every season, the call remains: Do not merely pass the food. Pass the peace. Because peace is not something we manufacture. It is something we carry. And the world desperately needs it.

### Peace Must Move Through Us

Peace was never meant to terminate with us. It must travel through us. This is one of the clearest implications of the gospel. If Christ reconciled us to God, then reconciliation becomes part of our assignment. Jesus said, "Blessed are the peacemakers" (Matthew 5:9). Not simply peace-lovers or peace-keepers but peacemakers.

Peace-making is active.

Intentional.

Costly.

It means stepping into conflict with humility. It means choosing forgiveness over retaliation. It means choosing understanding over assumption. It means carrying the tone of Christ into fractured spaces. This matters in marriage.

In parenting.

In leadership.

In friendship.

In church.

In public witness.

Peace-shaped people do not escalate chaos. They absorb it differently. They carry a stabilizing presence. Not because they are naturally calm. But because Christ reigns within them. This is one of the church's greatest witness opportunities in a divided world.

A peaceful people become a prophetic people. Because peace stands out in chaos. Wholeness stands out in fragmentation. Reconciliation stands out in division. And when believers carry peace into broken spaces, they become visible evidence of the kingdom of God. That is part of what it means to be light. Peace is not weak. Peace is kingdom strength under surrender.

## The Reign of Peace

Jesus makes us whole. And whole people help heal broken places. That is the work of peace. Not perfection. Wholeness. Not escape. Presence. Not the absence of trouble. But the reign of Christ in the middle of it.

That is shalom.

Peace that reigns in us must eventually shape the places we live most closely—our homes, our marriages, and our children. Peace was never meant to remain private. The peace Christ establishes in us must shape the places closest to us—our homes, our marriages, and our children. God's peace was never meant to stop with us.

## Chapter 4 Reflection Guide

### Reflect

1. What currently feels chaotic in your life—internally or externally?

2. When pressure rises, what usually governs your heart first: fear, anger, anxiety, control, or the peace of Christ?

3. Where have you confused the absence of conflict with true biblical peace (shalom)?

4. Are there unresolved places in your life where God wants to restore wholeness—not just calm?

5. What would it look like for the peace of Christ to "rule" in your heart this week?

---

**Respond**

Identify one area of internal unrest in your life right now.

Name it specifically.

A relationship.

A fear.

A financial burden.

A future uncertainty.

Write it down.

Then pray over it each day this week using one simple phrase:

**"Prince of Peace, reign here."**

Do not just ask for the problem to leave.

Invite Christ to rule there.

---

**Pray**

Lord Jesus,

You are my peace.

Not just the giver of peace—but peace itself.

Forgive me for allowing fear, anxiety, and chaos to govern my heart.

Teach me to let Your peace rule in me.

Bring wholeness to the fractured places in my life.

Restore what has been disordered by fear, sin, or pain.

Help me trust You in the storm and rest in Your nearness.

Let Your peace reign over my thoughts, my emotions, my relationships, and my future.

Make me whole in Your presence.

In Jesus' name, amen.

# Chapter 5
# Good News for My Family

*The presence of God in the home is not built through perfect moments, but through faithful rhythms of prayer, rest, worship, and obedience.*

The lights were off. The water was gone. Our baby was sick. And there was nothing we could do. I was about to learn a lesson I was not prepared for.

God used Nepal to teach me lessons I could not have learned any other way. Not through theory. Through hardship. Before one of the deepest crises our family would face, God taught us an earlier lesson about obedience.

Nepal was going through what they called *load shedding*. Electricity was rationed across the city. Different parts of the city received electricity only during assigned hours. At that time, our family's allotted electricity came from midnight until four in the morning.

And in Kathmandu, electricity meant more than light. Our water system depended on it. Water had to be pumped from the ground tank to the rooftop tank so gravity could distribute it through the house.

One night, exhausted from ministry and parenting, we slept through our electricity window. That meant no water and no stored water. And that morning, our eight-month-old daughter became violently sick. She vomited and soiled herself.

We woke up to chaos.

No lights.

No running water.

No practical way to care for her.

We used our cell phone lights just to see. We reached for wet cloths to clean her, only to realize there was no water available until the next electricity cycle later that evening.

It felt absurd, humiliating, and defeating. I remember feeling like I could not even fulfill the most basic responsibility as a father. And later that morning, I was scheduled to lead ministry in one of the international churches.

How could I stand before people and lead spiritually when I could not even clean my own child? I remember sitting with Bethany, discouraged, talking through the morning. I asked her if maybe we should leave. Go to Bangkok. Take a break. Get a hot shower. Recover. Reset. Escape the difficulty. And then Bethany looked at me with a resolve I will never forget. She said:

**"No. We should stay. God has not called us to live a life of ease. He has called us to obedience."**

That sentence became our family motto. And it has shaped our household ever since. God has not called us to what is easy. He has called us to obedience. That is family discipleship. It is messy. It is not the pursuit of comfort but the pursuit of faithfulness. Long before I understood it theologically, I was learning it domestically: God forms people in the ordinary spaces of home.

For many believers, faith is largely externalized—measured by church attendance and Sunday worship. But the deepest formation of faith does not happen in church services. It happens at home. Around tables. In routines. In interruptions. In ordinary moments.

The household is one of God's primary environments of formation. Long before there was temple, synagogue, or church, there was household. And if the presence of God cannot shape a home, it will struggle to shape anything else.

## Presence Begins at Home

Peace that remains private is incomplete. God intends His peace to shape homes. The presence of God was never meant to remain confined to sanctuaries. It was always meant to come home. The garden itself was a household environment. God walked with humanity in daily fellowship (Genesis 3:8). Presence was domestic before it was institutional.

Later, in Deuteronomy 6, God instructed Israel: Teach these things to your children. Talk of them when you sit. When you walk. When you lie down. When you rise. Faith was never meant to be occasional. It was rhythmic. Embedded. Repeated. Formative.

The home was always the primary training ground. The church supports it. But the home sustains it.

### Every Home Has a Liturgy

Whether intentional or not, every home has a liturgy. Not necessarily formal prayers or written readings, but repeated practices that shape what a family loves, fears, values, and expects. A liturgy is simply repeated formation.

What happens repeatedly becomes formative. Every household is being discipled by repetition. Some homes are discipled by hurry. Schedules dominate. Conversations are rushed. Meals are fragmented. Attention is divided. Presence is thin.

Other homes are discipled by entertainment. Screens dominate. Silence is filled. Boredom is avoided. Attention is outsourced. And slowly, formation is happening. Not because anyone intended it. But because repetition always teaches.

**This is why intentional rhythms matter. Not because routines save us. But because routines shape us.**

When prayer becomes normal, children learn dependence.
When Scripture becomes normal, children learn truth.
When worship becomes normal, children learn surrender.
When confession becomes normal, children learn humility.

When forgiveness becomes normal, children learn grace. Homes are always teaching. The question is never whether formation is happening. The question is what kind of formation is happening. That is why Christian households must become intentional. Not rigid. Intentional.

**Families Are Formed by Rhythm**

What we repeat forms us. Not what we occasionally celebrate. Rhythm shapes reality. In our home, we have built rhythms intentionally. Morning devotions. Scripture memory. Singing praise. Nightly prayer with every child. Family prayer. Advent Jesse Tree readings each Christmas season. Shared prayer over meals. Sabbath preparation.

These practices are not about performance. They are about formation. We are not always perfect. Our Sabbath is not always kept with precision. But we keep returning to it.

Returning matters. Consistency matters. Presence grows in repeated return. This is especially true in family life. Because children are not primarily shaped by what parents teach. They are shaped by what parents repeat.

Children inhale what parents normalize. If hurry is normalized, they inherit hurry. If anxiety is normalized, they inherit anxiety. If prayer is normalized, they inherit prayer. If peace is normalized, they inherit peace. If presence is normalized, they inherit presence. Joshua's declaration—"As for me and my house, we will serve the Lord"—was not merely a family slogan; it was covenantal theology. Families mattered deeply in the biblical imagination. Even in Acts 16, salvation repeatedly moves through households, reminding us that God often works relationally and generationally.

### Repetition Builds Memory

One of the great gifts of repeated spiritual rhythms is memory. Repetition builds memory into the soul. This is one of the reasons God built repetition into Israel's life.

Feasts.

Sabbaths.

Festivals.

Prayers.

Meals.

Storytelling.

Repeated acts of remembrance. Why? Because memory sustains faith. When life becomes hard, people fall back on what has been deeply formed in them. Not merely what they once heard. What they have repeatedly practiced.

This is especially true for children.

Children may not remember every lesson. But they will remember patterns. They will remember whether prayer mattered. Whether worship mattered. Whether church mattered. Whether Scripture mattered. Whether repentance happened. Whether forgiveness was practiced.

They will remember the emotional climate of the home. And memory becomes inheritance. This is one of the reasons our family keeps Advent rhythms each year through Jesse Tree readings. Not because ritual is the goal. But because memory matters.

We are building spiritual memory. Anchoring the story of God into the story of our family. That is discipleship. Not occasional inspiration. Repeated remembrance.

## Sabbath Jobs and Sacred Preparation

In our family, even rest requires preparation. We call them *Sabbath jobs*—practical tasks completed ahead of Sabbath so that rest can be protected. That matters because rest is never accidental; it is intentional. Sabbath is not merely the absence of work but the intentional cultivation of holy rest.

Walter Brueggemann argues that Sabbath is an act of resistance—a refusal to live unreflectively within systems of endless hurry, production, and self-reliance. It resists the kind of life God never intended humanity to bear. Preparation, then, becomes an act of discipleship.

As Brueggemann writes, "the celebration of Sabbath is an act of both resistance and alternative."[4] It resists the anxiety-driven systems that measure human worth by productivity and possession. When we choose to rest, we declare defiance against the cultural powers that attempt to define us by what we produce or consume. We refuse to become commodities. Instead, we embrace a life tethered to God through rest, mercy, and covenantal dependence.

Many assume Sabbath is passive. That is one of its great misunderstandings. Sabbath is not passive; it is structured surrender. It requires trust—trust that the world continues turning when we stop, trust that provision does not depend entirely on our striving, and trust that God sustains what we cannot control. When children participate in the preparation for Sabbath, they learn that rest is not laziness. It is holiness.

## Presence in Crisis

When our son stopped eating for twenty-five days, our family was tested. Prayer intensified. Fear expanded. At first, we were convinced he would be healed. But as the days stretched on, certainty became harder to maintain. Faith under delay is different than faith under immediacy.

It is one thing to believe for healing. It is another to believe while watching your child weaken. Bethany and I prayed together, continually. And somewhere in that wilderness,

---

[4] Walter Brueggemann, *Sabbath as Resistance: Saying No to the Culture of Now* (John Knox Press, 2017), 92.

God confronted me. Would I serve Him without bargaining? Would I remain faithful if the answer I wanted never came? And in that place, the Spirit gave me a melody. Simple. Persistent. Repeated in my heart:

**I'll serve You, no bargaining.**
**My life is my offering.**

That became worship in suffering. And worship became stability. Presence held us together. That is what families need. Not perfect outcomes. Present faithfulness.

### Obedience Over Ease

Every family builds around a governing value. Comfort. Success. Security. Convenience. But Christian households must build around obedience. Comfort is unstable. Obedience is rooted. Comfort cannot sustain suffering. Obedience can.

Our family motto emerged in weakness. But it continues in strength: God has not called us to what is easy. He has called us to obedience. That conviction has shaped how we parent. How we schedule. How we rest. How we pray. How we suffer. And how we continue.

### Presence Creates Witness

Households shaped by presence become visible. Not perfect. Visible. Peace, forgiveness, and prayer become visible. Children learn what God looks like by watching their parents respond to life.

Formation is often transferred before it is taught. Timothy inherited faith from his mother and grandmother (2 Timothy 1:5). Faith travels relationally. Presence does too. This is the hope: That homes become outposts of God's presence. Not because everything goes right. But because God remains near.

**What Children Learn from Watching**

Children are extraordinary observers. They see more than we think. And they absorb more than we realize. They watch

how we respond to inconvenience. How we handle disappointment. How we speak to one another. How we treat strangers. How we handle conflict. How we repent. How we recover. How we worship. How we suffer.

They are watching theology in motion. This is one of the most sobering realities of parenting. Because children often learn God before they understand doctrine. They interpret Him through the emotional and spiritual atmosphere of the home.

That does not mean parents must be perfect. Thank God. But it does mean parents must be honest.

Quick to repent.

Quick to forgive.

Quick to return.

Children do not need flawless parents. They need faithful ones. Parents who keep returning to Jesus. Parents who keep practicing surrender. Parents who keep choosing obedience over ease. And over time, that faithfulness becomes believable. Not because it was preached. Because it was witnessed.

This is part of what Paul saw in Timothy. Faith was embodied in his mother and grandmother before it was strengthened in him (2 Timothy 1:5). Faith often travels relationally. Presence does too.

### The Invitation Home

Your home does not have to be impressive to host God's presence. It does not have to be large. Perfect. Peaceful. Or polished. It simply must be surrendered.

Presence grows where surrender lives. And often the most powerful transformation happens not in grand spiritual moments—but in ordinary obedience. Morning prayers. Shared meals. Simple songs. Nightly blessings. Prepared rest. Repeated faithfulness.

This is good news for families. God does not only visit churches. He inhabits households. And when His presence fills a home, formation deepens. The rhythms that shape a household also shape the soul.

What forms a family eventually forms the individual. The rhythms of the home become the habits of the soul. Beneath every family rhythm is a deeper reality: the Spirit of God Himself is quietly at work forming Christ in us.

**Chapter 5 Reflection Guide**

**Reflect**

1. What rhythms currently shape your home (intentional or unintentional)?

2. If your household culture could be described in three words, what would they be?

3. What spiritual habits are your children, spouse, or family learning from what you repeat?

4. Is your home structured more around comfort and convenience—or around faithfulness and presence?

5. What is one area where God may be inviting your household into greater obedience?

---

**Respond**

Choose one spiritual rhythm to strengthen in your household this week.

Examples:

- prayer at meals
- nightly prayer
- family worship
- Scripture reading
- Sabbath preparation
- Sabbath rest
- intentional blessing over your children

Do not try to change everything.

Choose one. Start small. Repeat faithfully.

Remember: Families are formed by what they repeat.

---

**Pray**

Lord,

thank You for the gift of my household.

Forgive me for the ways I have allowed hurry, distraction, or convenience to shape our home more than Your presence.

Help me build a home marked by peace, prayer, obedience, and rest.

Teach us to practice Your presence in ordinary moments.

Strengthen our family rhythms and help us remain faithful in small things.

Give me wisdom to lead with humility and love.

Let our home become a place where Your presence is welcomed and where faith is formed.

Make our household a place of peace and obedience.

In Jesus' name, amen.

# Chapter 6
# Formed by the Spirit

*Holy Spirit does not simply empower us for what we do; He forms us for who we become.*

I was young, capable, and more confident than I should have been. Like many young leaders, I wanted to matter. I wanted to be effective. I wanted to make an impact. And if I'm honest, I also wanted to be seen as important. By God's grace, I had experienced success in several ministry areas early on. People were responding. Ministry was growing. Doors were opening.

But success has a way of feeding confidence. And if left unchecked, confidence can quietly become arrogance. That happened to me. I was leading in ministry and had become a little too sure of myself. One day, in what I thought was a helpful conversation, I began telling an older minister how they could "do better" in their ministry. At least that's how I framed it in my mind. Helpful. Constructive.

But what I could not see in that moment was how my words sounded coming from a freshly graduated college kid speaking to someone who had been laboring in ministry for years. My "helpful suggestions" sounded less like wisdom and more like arrogance. And they responded in a way I did not expect. They simply offered to let me take over their responsibilities immediately. That moment hit me hard.

Suddenly, I saw it.

Not my wisdom. My pride. Not my insight. My immaturity. And almost immediately, the Holy Spirit corrected me. Not harshly. Clearly. He exposed something in me that needed pruning: pride, self-importance, and premature confidence.

That moment taught me something essential: The Holy Spirit does not only comfort us. He confronts us. Because He loves us. He corrects what He intends to mature. And often the Spirit's greatest work in us is not making us powerful, but making us holy.

**Presence Produces the Character of Christ**

The rhythms that shape our homes are also the rhythms through which the Spirit shapes us. The presence of God does not merely comfort us. It changes us. And the primary means of that transformation is the Holy Spirit.

One of the great misunderstandings in Pentecostal Christianity is reducing the Holy Spirit to moments. Moments of power, emotion, manifestation, and encounter.

And while all of those can be real, the ministry of the Holy Spirit is far deeper than isolated spiritual moments. The

Holy Spirit is not merely the God of moments. He is the God of formation. He forms Christ in us.

The Spirit does not simply touch us. He transforms us. This matters because many believers want the power of the Spirit without the process of the Spirit. But Scripture consistently ties presence to transformation. The presence of God is not merely for experience. It is for growth.

### The Holy Spirit Is the Presence of God

Before we can understand spiritual formation, we must understand who the Holy Spirit is. The Holy Spirit is not an impersonal force. Not energy. Not intuition. Not emotional sensation. He is God. Personal. Present. Active.

Jesus says: "And I will ask the Father, and he will give you another Helper..." (John 14:16–17). The Spirit is the ongoing presence of God among His people. This is the great gift of the new covenant: God does not merely dwell near us. He dwells in us. That changes everything.

When COVID pneumonia placed me in the hospital for a week, isolation created space for reflection. Illness reveals what sustains you. In that hospital room, God's presence was not abstract. It was sustaining. When you have been carried by His presence in weakness, you emerge changed.

Because spiritual growth is not merely behavior modification. It is divine participation. God Himself is present within the believer—not observing from a distance. Forming from within.

Gordon Fee in, *Paul, the Spirit, and the People of God*, emphasizes that the Spirit is not merely an empowering force for ministry, but the personal presence of God actively forming the people of God into the likeness of Christ.[5]

### The Spirit Is Not Your Conscience

Many Christians confuse inner impressions with the Holy Spirit. But conscience and Spirit are not the same. Conscience can be shaped by culture and experience. It can be weak. It can be misinformed. It can be corrupted. But the Holy Spirit is holy.

He does not merely reflect internal psychology. He reveals divine truth. Jesus called Him the Spirit of truth (John 16:13). And His ministry always aligns with Scripture. He never contradicts the Word He inspired. This is essential.

Not every thought is divine. Not every feeling is revelation. Not every impulse is the Spirit. Discernment matters. The Spirit leads us into truth. Not self-justification. Not emotional convenience. Truth.

### The Spirit Is Our Counselor

Jesus said it was to our advantage that He go away. That is astonishing. How could the physical departure of Jesus be advantageous? Because the Spirit would come. Not beside us. Within us.

---

[5] Gordon Fee, *Paul, the Spirit, and the People of God* (Baker Academics, 2023), 20.

Jesus describes Him as Advocate. Counselor. Helper. Guide (John 16:7–14). The Spirit counsels us. Corrects us. Convicts us. Leads us. Comforts us. He is not merely present in crisis. He is present in process.

That distinction matters. Many people seek God only when life collapses. But the Spirit walks with us daily. In decisions. Relationships. Maturity. Obedience. He is not emergency support. Holy Spirit is daily companionship.

**The Nurturing Presence of God**

The Holy Spirit nurtures. Not in sentimentality. But in sanctification. Paul says we can grieve the Spirit (Ephesians 4:30). That means relationship. Personality. Sensitivity. He is not an impersonal power.

He is relationally involved. He nurtures what Christ is building. This is important for understanding spiritual growth. Growth is not merely discipline. It is cooperation. We cooperate with the nurturing work of the Spirit. He prunes, shapes, convicts, and strengthens us.

And all of it is love. Even conviction is love. Because conviction protects sanctification. One of the ways the Holy Spirit forms us is through correction. Not condemnation. Correction. There is a difference. Condemnation pushes us away. Correction pulls us closer. And often, correction comes through exposing what we could not see in ourselves.

It is making us humble.

Formation is not always dramatic. Sometimes it looks like embarrassment. Repentance. And learning to listen more than speak. That is the nurturing work of the Spirit. He shapes us not only through victories—but through correction.

### The Spirit Produces What We Cannot

Perhaps the clearest evidence of the Spirit's work is fruit. Paul writes: "The fruit of the Spirit is..." (Galatians 5:22–23). Notice the language. Fruit is produced. Not manufactured. Not performed. Produced.

This is crucial.

The Christian life is not self-powered morality. It is Spirit-produced character. Love. Joy. Peace. Patience. Kindness. Goodness. Faithfulness. Gentleness. Self-control. These are not personality traits. They are evidence of divine presence. They reveal the character of Christ.

That is the point.

The Spirit forms the character of Jesus in us. What makes the church different is not attendance or affiliation, but transformation. In John 15, Jesus teaches that fruit grows through abiding, not striving. Branches do not strain to bear fruit; they remain connected to the vine. Fruit is not produced by effort alone but by abiding presence.

### Fruit Shows Up in Ordinary Places

One of the misunderstandings about spiritual fruit is assuming it appears primarily in spiritual settings. Church. Prayer meetings. Worship services. Ministry moments. But fruit is usually revealed in ordinary life.

Patience is not primarily proven in worship. It is proven in interruption. Kindness is not proven in a prayer gathering. It is proven in conflict. Self-control is not proven when life is easy. It is proven when temptation is strong. Gentleness is not proven in comfort.

It is proven in confrontation. This matters because many believers assess their spiritual maturity in ideal settings. But maturity is usually exposed in inconvenient ones. How do you respond when plans collapse? When people disappoint you? When stress rises? When criticism comes? When the answer is delayed? That is often where fruit becomes visible.

The Holy Spirit forms us for real life.

Not merely church life. And this is good news. Because it means every interruption becomes an opportunity for formation. Every inconvenience becomes training. Every frustration becomes invitation. Not because difficulty is good in itself. But because the Spirit uses real life to reveal what is still being formed.

### Presence Before Power

Pentecostals rightly celebrate the power of the Spirit. And we should. But power without character is dangerous.

Gifting without fruit is unstable. Anointing without formation is unsustainable. The Spirit who empowers ministry also forms maturity. These cannot be separated.

Power serves mission. Fruit sustains mission. Both matter. But fruit reveals depth. Jesus said we would know people by their fruit (Matthew 7:16). Not their gifting. Their fruit. That is sobering. Because gifts can impress. Fruit reveals.

## Power Must Be Carried Well

Power is a gift. But gifts require maturity to carry them well. This is one of the tensions in Pentecostal life. God can empower quickly. But character often develops slowly.

And if power outpaces character, instability follows. This is why formation matters so deeply. Because what the Spirit gives, the soul must be able to carry.

Influence.

Responsibility.

Opportunity.

Authority.

Visibility.

All of it. Jesus Himself spent thirty years in hidden formation before three years of visible ministry. That matters. Preparation mattered. Formation mattered. Hiddenness mattered. And if the Son of God embraced process, how much more should we?

This is not meant to discourage hunger for spiritual power. Quite the opposite. Seek all that God has. Receive all He gives. Walk in gifts. Move in faith. Minister boldly. But let formation keep pace with empowerment.

Because sustainable ministry requires both. Power may open doors. Character keeps you standing once they open.

### The Slow Work of Formation

Fruit takes time. Trees do not mature overnight. Neither do believers. Formation is slow. Often hidden. Sometimes frustrating. But deeply necessary. God is patient.

And so must we be.

Many believers become discouraged because they want instant transformation. But the Spirit works organically. Steadily. Faithfully. Like roots deepening before fruit appears. Presence precedes production. The more we abide, the more fruit emerges. We cooperate with the Spirit through:

- surrender
- repentance
- attentiveness
- obedience
- confession
- Scripture
- prayer

### The Spirit Meets Us in Weakness

One of the most comforting realities about the Holy Spirit is that He does not wait for strength before He works. He often begins in weakness. Paul writes in Romans 8 that the Spirit helps us in our weakness.

Not after weakness.

In weakness.

That matters. Because many believers feel disqualified by their weakness. Their limitations.

Their failures. Their inconsistencies. But weakness is not where the Spirit withdraws. It is often where He works most deeply.

I have seen this repeatedly in my own life. Illness taught me that. Hospital rooms taught me that. Loss taught me that. Weakness strips away illusion. It exposes what we trust. What we fear. What we build on.

And often, in weakness, the Spirit becomes clearer because the distractions become fewer. We discover that His sustaining presence is not theoretical. It is experiential. This is one of the hidden gifts of weakness. It teaches dependence. And dependence is fertile ground for formation.

Strength often hides self-reliance. Weakness often exposes it. And where self-reliance is exposed, surrender becomes possible. That is often where formation deepens. Not in strength. In surrender.

**Becoming Like Christ**

The ultimate goal of the Spirit's work is Christlikeness. Not spiritual weirdness. Not emotional intensity. Christlikeness. Paul says we are transformed from glory to glory by the Spirit (2 Corinthians 3:18). Transformation is the evidence of presence.

As Richard Foster in *Celebration of Discipline* notes, spiritual disciplines do not earn God's presence; they place us where His transforming work can be received.[6]

The question is not: Did I feel something? The deeper question is: Am I becoming like Jesus? More patient? More loving? More peaceful? More faithful? That is formation. And that is the work of the Spirit.

**Spirit baptism empowers mission.**

Pentecostals emphasize the empowering work of Spirit baptism for testifying and declaring the gospel. This empowerment does not replace formation; it strengthens it. The Spirit fills us for witness and forms us for endurance. Power launches mission. Fruit sustains what power begins. It is here that the fruit of abiding in Jesus comes along and sustains you.

---

[6] Richard Foster, *Celebration of Discipline: The Path to Spiritual Growth* (HarperSanFransico, 2018), 8.

**The Invitation**

The Holy Spirit is not merely the God of dramatic moments. He is the God of daily formation. He is present—counseling, correcting, nurturing, producing, transforming. And if we will yield ourselves to Him, He will produce what we cannot manufacture. The character and power of Christ. This is the invitation: Not merely to experience His presence. But to be formed by it. Because the goal of presence is not just encounter. It is transformation.

I want to challenge you to open yourself up to encountering Holy Spirit's presence. Ask yourself honestly, "Am I living in the fullness of all that Jesus promised through His Spirit?" If your answer is no, simply ask Jesus to give you everything that He has promised you. Then, simply receive from the Spirit of Jesus what He has promised.

Formation always moves outward. The Spirit does not form us merely for ourselves. He forms us for the world. He does not mold us for isolation. He does it to move us outward. A life shaped by the Spirit becomes visible in the way we love, serve, and shine.

## Chapter 6 Reflection Guide

### Reflect

1. When you think about the Holy Spirit, do you primarily think of power, gifts, and moments—or formation, character, and daily guidance?

2. Which fruit of the Spirit (love, joy, peace, patience, kindness, goodness, faithfulness, gentleness, self-control) is strongest in your life right now?

3. Which fruit feels weakest or most underdeveloped?

4. Are there areas where you are asking God for greater spiritual power while resisting His work of character formation?

5. Where might the Holy Spirit be convicting, pruning, or shaping you right now?

---

### Respond

Read through the fruit of the Spirit in Galatians 5:22–23.

Choose one fruit that you sense the Holy Spirit wants to strengthen in you right now.

Write it down.

Then ask: What would this fruit look like in my actual life this week?

Be specific. If patience: Where? With whom?

If self-control: In what area?

If kindness: Toward whom?

Practice cooperation with the Spirit. Not performance. Cooperation.

---

**Pray**

Holy Spirit,

thank You for living in me and walking with me.

Forgive me for the times I have desired power without surrender, gifting without maturity, or spiritual experience without transformation.

Form the character of Christ in me.

Grow Your fruit in my life.

Prune what needs pruning.

Correct what needs correcting.

Strengthen what is weak.

Teach me to cooperate with Your work in me.

Make me more loving, more faithful, more peaceful, and more like Jesus.

Let my life reflect not just Your power, but Your presence.

In Jesus' name, amen.

# Part III

# Mission & Devotion

# Chapter 7
# Be Light

*People who live near God begin seeing people differently.*

I have made it a habit to learn the names of the people serving my table. I genuinely love talking to servers. Not because I need exceptional service, but because I want to see the person beyond the role. Hospitality work can be invisible work. People often see the task but miss the person. So I have made it a personal practice to learn their name, use it in conversation, and treat them like they matter—because they do.

A few years ago, I added another simple practice. Before the meal, I would ask: “Is there anything I can pray for you about? I’m a Christian, and I’m going to pray for my meal anyway. I’d love to pray for you too.”

It’s a small question. But it opens big doors. Over the years, this simple practice has led to countless meaningful conversations.

One of the first times I started doing this, I noticed a tattoo on my server’s arm. It was a small, delicate flower. And I felt the Holy Spirit draw my attention to it. Not in some overwhelming dramatic way. Just a gentle inner nudge: Ask about that.

So I did.

I asked her about the tattoo.

And what began as a small conversation quickly opened into something much deeper. She began telling me the story behind it. Family. Pain. Conflict. Struggles. Things she was carrying quietly while serving tables and smiling through her shift. And suddenly, what began as dinner became ministry.

I usually try to carry a small New Testament with me for moments like that. That day, I had one. Before I left, I wrote her name in it and gave it to her. She teared up. I was able to pray for her right there and place the Scriptures into her hands. And it all started because I paid attention.

A small tattoo.

A small nudge.

A simple question.

That's often how the Holy Spirit works. Not always through dramatic interruption. Often through attentive obedience. Spirit-aware people learn to notice. To listen. To respond. And sometimes the smallest moments become the holiest ones. People who live near God begin seeing people differently

**Attention Is a Spiritual Discipline**

One of the first things the presence of God changes is what we notice. Or perhaps more accurately, who we notice. Much of modern life trains us toward distraction. We move quickly. We consume quickly. We scroll quickly. We speak quickly. We often move through crowds of people without truly seeing anyone.

But the Spirit slows our attention. He teaches us to notice.

Names.

Faces.

Pain.

Needs.

Openings.

Interruptions.

This matters because love begins with attention. You cannot love what you refuse to notice. And many divine appointments are hidden inside ordinary moments of attention. Jesus was never hurried past people.

He noticed Zacchaeus in a tree.

The bleeding woman in a crowd.

Blind Bartimaeus on the roadside.

The widow at the temple.

The disciples often missed what Jesus noticed. But Jesus noticed people. And presence-shaped people begin noticing people too. This is not complicated. But it is deeply spiritual. To notice someone is often the first act of love. And often the first step of witness.

**Presence for the Neighborhood**

The Spirit does not form us merely for personal growth. He forms us so Christ can be seen through us. The Christian life was never designed to end with personal transformation.

It was always meant to move outward.

We do not love our neighbors to earn God's presence. We love because we have been shaped by it. The presence of God is never merely private. It is missional. God forms us so He can send us. This is one of the central truths of Scripture: Love for God always moves toward love for people. Jesus reduced the entire law into two commands:

Love God.

Love your neighbor.

That's it. Everything else hangs there. Jesus summarized the whole law in two commandments: love God and love your neighbor (Matthew 22:37–40). These are not separate commands. They are connected. Love for God naturally overflows into love for neighbor. Timothy Keller, in *Generous Justice* reminds us that love of neighbor is one of the clearest evidences of genuine love for God.[7] And where that love flows, light appears.

### Life's Purpose Begins with Loving God

Many people spend their lives asking: What is my purpose? What am I supposed to do? What is God's will? Jesus simplifies what we complicate.

Love God and love people.

Life's deepest purpose is relational before it is vocational. Before assignment, calling, or ministry—there is relationship. To know God. To love God.

Paul captured this when he wrote: "I count everything as loss because of the surpassing worth of knowing Christ" (Philippians 3:8). Everything flows from there. Christian life is not primarily built on activity. It is built on intimacy. Everything else follows. Ministry follows. Mission follows. Witness follows. Light follows. But first: Love God.

### To Love God, You Must Be Born of God

Love for God is not natural. It is supernatural. Jesus told Nicodemus: "You must be born again" (John 3:3). This is crucial. Christianity is not behavior modification.

---

[7] Timothy Keller, *Generous Justice: How God's Grace Makes Us Just*, (Dutton, 2010), 104.

It is new birth.

Because we cannot truly love God until God changes our hearts. Love for God begins where new life begins. And new life changes everything. New affections. New desires. New loyalties. New vision. New love. And once that love takes root, it cannot stay hidden. In John 1:14 , John writes that the Word became flesh. This matters because: Our witness is incarnational. Not merely informational. Before the gospel was preached, it was embodied.

## Be Light

Jesus shifts from inward love to outward witness. “You are the light of the world” (Matthew 5:14–16). Notice: Jesus does not say you *have* light. He says you *are* light. Identity before activity. This is presence theology. Because light is what happens when presence fills a life. Just as the moon reflects the sun, believers reflect Christ. That is witness. Not perfection. Reflection. And the world desperately needs that light. Not because the church is flawless. But because Christ is.

## Who Is My Neighbor?

Jesus radically expanded this question. Neighbor is not merely proximity. Neighbor is anyone God places in your path. The coworker. The classmate. The server. The literal next-door neighbor. The stranger. The overlooked.

Anyone God places in my path.

This changes evangelism. Evangelism is not merely an event. It is a lifestyle of attention. God-conscious people pay attention.

## Incarnational Witness

One of the greatest truths of the gospel is that God came near. He did not save us from a distance. He entered our world. John says, "The Word became flesh and dwelt among us" (John 1:14).

That is incarnation.

Presence moving toward people. This matters because our witness follows the same pattern. Christian witness is incarnational. Not merely informational. We do not simply deliver truths. We embody them. We enter people's world.

We listen.

We care.

We sit in pain.

We enter tension.

We make room for struggle.

This is often what makes witness believable. Not argument. Presence. People are far more likely to receive truth from someone who has first embodied love.

This is why hospitality matters. Listening matters. Serving matters. Showing up matters. Presence gives credibility to proclamation. Not because love replaces truth. But because love prepares the soil for truth.

That is what Jesus did. He came near. And we are called to do the same.

## Tell Jesus About Your Neighbor

Before telling your neighbor about Jesus—tell Jesus about your neighbor. Prayer precedes witness. James reminds us that the prayer of a righteous person has great power (James 5:16). Prayer changes people. But prayer also changes us. It aligns our hearts with God's heart. Prayer changes how we see people and deepens compassion.

In your ministry practice, this became practical: Know their name. Pray their name. Names matter because people matter. And prayer makes people visible. Not projects. People.

## Witness Requires Courage

At some point, witness moves from internal compassion to external courage. This is where many believers hesitate. Not because they do not care. But because fear gets involved.

What if they reject me?

What if it gets awkward?

What if I say it wrong?

What if they are offended?

Those fears are real. But courage is not the absence of fear. It is obedience in the presence of fear. This is one of the great works of the Holy Spirit. He does not merely give compassion. He gives boldness.

In Acts 4, after persecution and pressure, the disciples prayed—not for safety, but for boldness. And the Spirit filled them. Why? Because witness requires courage. And courage grows through practice.

Small conversations.

Small prayers.

Small invitations.

Small acts of obedience.

Over time, courage grows. Not because fear disappears. But because love becomes stronger than fear. This is important to remember: You are not responsible for results. Only faithfulness. God handles hearts. You carry witness. That frees us. We do not convert anyone.

We testify.

We love.

We speak. And God moves.

### Tell Jesus Their Need

Prayer deepens awareness. As we pray, we begin seeing differently. Needs become visible. Pain becomes visible. Opportunity becomes visible. Love becomes practical. People do not care how much we know until they know how much we care. That's not merely cliché. It's incarnational. Jesus entered people's pain. And so do we. Presence-shaped people become attentive to wounds.

### Tell Jesus Their Potential

Jesus saw beyond people's past. Beyond labels. Beyond failures. Beyond reputation. He saw potential and calling. This is how presence changes vision. Prayer helps us see people as God sees them. Not merely what they are. But what they may become. That changes evangelism. We stop writing people off. Because God does not.

### Tell Your Neighbor About Jesus

At some point, witness must become verbal. Presence matters. Love matters. Service matters. But proclamation matters too. Light must be visible. Jesus said lamps are meant to shine. Not hide. Your story matters.

A simple testimony often follows three movements: life before Christ, the moment Christ met you, and the life He is shaping now.

Before Christ:

What was broken? What was empty? What was lost? Not glorifying sin. Just honest.

Encounter with Christ:

What happened? Why did you surrender? How did Christ meet you? That moment matters.

Life in Christ:

What is God doing now? How is He changing you? How is He sustaining you? People need living testimony. Not polished theology. Living witness.

**The Neighborhood Needs the Light**

The world does not need a hidden church. It needs a visible church. Not just loud. Visible. Present. Faithful. Loving. Luminous. Jesus said: “The light shines in the darkness...” (John 1:5). Darkness does not overcome light. Light overcomes darkness.

That is our calling. Not simply to curse darkness. Shine. Love. Pray. Serve. Speak. Witness.

**Light the Night**

There is darkness everywhere—fear, confusion, addiction, brokenness, loneliness. But light still works. One candle changes a room. One witness changes a conversation. One prayer changes a heart. One act of love changes a life. That is the power of presence.

Presence becomes peace. Peace becomes formation. Formation becomes witness. And witness becomes light. That is the movement of the Christian life. Love God. Be light. And trust that God will use your life to bring His presence into the neighborhood. We cannot reflect the Light if we drift from the Light Himself.

Witness is not the end goal of the Christian life. It is the overflow of a life rooted in God's presence. And sustaining that life requires intentional devotion.

## Chapter 7 Reflection Guide

### Reflect

1. Is my love for God active and growing—or has it become routine and familiar?

2. Does my daily life create enough space for God's presence to shape how I see people?

3. When I encounter people in need, am I attentive to the Holy Spirit's prompting—or distracted by my own agenda?

4. Who in my life might God be inviting me to see differently—not as an interruption, but as an assignment?

5. If my life is meant to be light, where is God asking me to shine more intentionally right now?

---

**Respond**

Choose one person in your life this week—a neighbor, coworker, friend, family member, or stranger God keeps bringing to mind.

For seven days:

Pray for them by name.

Pray for their needs.

Pray for their future in Christ.

Then ask the Holy Spirit:

**How can I love this person in a practical way this week?**

Listen. Act. Be present. Be light.

---

**Pray**

Lord,

thank You for loving me and drawing me near to Yourself.

Deepen my love for You and keep my heart tender toward Your presence.

Forgive me for the ways distraction, routine, or selfishness have dulled my awareness of the people around me.

Open my eyes to see others the way You see them.

Fill me with Your love so fully that it overflows into my relationships and my neighborhood.

Help me to be present, attentive, and obedient to Your leading.

Make my life a light that points others to You.

Use me to carry Your presence into the places You have assigned me.

In Jesus' name, amen.

# Chapter 8
# Becoming People of His Presence

*Presence is not merely something we encounter. It is the life we choose.*

Becoming a person of God's presence does not happen accidentally. It is cultivated intentionally and repeated daily. God gives Himself freely, but awareness of His nearness must be cultivated. This is where many believers misunderstand the Christian life. They assume proximity to God automatically produces maturity.

It does not.

To become people of His presence means learning to live consciously aware of God. Not occasionally. Consciously. In every decision. Every movement. Every response. Every thought.

Presence must be practiced. Not because God is absent. But because our awareness is inconsistent. In *The Practice of the Presence of God*, Brother Lawrence teaches that the presence of God is cultivated in ordinary faithfulness—that even common tasks can become communion when done with awareness of God. Presence is both gift and pursuit. [8]

One of the old illustrations used in revival circles was this: Live like you have a dove on your shoulder.

Move carefully.

Speak carefully.

Act carefully.

Not out of fear. Out of awareness. The dove represents Holy Spirit—a picture of spiritual sensitivity. A life that moves with God in mind. A person of His presence asks: What pleases Him? What grieves Him? What honors Him? What aligns with His design?

This is not legalism. It is love.

That distinction matters. Many people hear words like holiness or devotion and think burden. Restriction. Pressure. But love changes how we see obedience. In marriage, faithfulness is not a burden when love is alive. I do not wake up every day needing to be convinced that faithfulness to my wife, Bethany, is the right thing.

I love her. I want to be faithful.

Faithfulness is not difficult when love is alive. It is delight. Even now, I am amazed she lets me love her. That

---

[8] Brother Lawrence, *The practice of the presence of God: The complete works of Brother Lawrence with notes and Scripture references* (Perieco Publishing, 2009), 50.

amazement fuels devotion. The same is true with God. We should never lose the wonder that God allows us access to His presence. That He welcomes us. Speaks to us. Walks with us. Forms us. This is not a chore. It is not boring. It is life. Devotion is not drudgery. It is delight.

### You Already Have as Much of God as You Want

Old revivalists used to say: "You can have as much of God as you want. In fact, you already do." That statement is uncomfortable because it removes excuses. It confronts the reality that desire makes room for devotion. How much room have we made? How much attention have we given? How much priority have we assigned? Becoming people of His presence requires honest inventory. Because God is not usually absent. We are distracted.

### What Dulls Awareness

What destroys awareness of God's presence? Not usually dramatic rebellion. Usually subtle erosion. Small compromises. Neglected prayer. Ignored Scripture. Unmanaged appetites. Distraction.

1 John warns of three rival affections: the lust of the flesh, the lust of the eyes, and the pride of life. These competing loves slowly erode awareness of God (1 John 2:16). These things compete for affection. Compete for focus. Compete

for devotion. They move to the front of the line. And when they do, awareness fades.

The dove on the shoulder gets forgotten.

Not because the Spirit leaves. But because competing loves grow louder. That is the danger. Presence is not often lost in catastrophe. It is often lost in neglect.

### Practices of Presence

Awareness must be cultivated. Presence is practiced through rhythms of fellowship. Prayer. Scripture. Worship. Stillness. Repentance. Gratitude. For me, that means daily prayer—not once, but multiple times throughout the day. Daily Scripture—not as obligation, but nourishment. Returning to the Word repeatedly.

Re-centering.

Re-aligning.

It also means limiting distractions. Phones. Social media. Digital noise. Not because technology is evil. But because attention is finite. And what captures attention shapes affection. In John 10:10, Jesus warns that the enemy comes to steal, kill, and destroy. Often what is stolen first is attention. And attention matters. Because communion grows where attention rests.

**A Rule of Life Protects What Matters**

One of the great challenges of spiritual life is that good intentions are rarely enough. Most believers want closeness with God. Want consistency. Want devotion. Want depth. But desire without structure often dissolves into inconsistency.

This is why a rule of life matters. A rule of life is simply a pattern of intentional rhythms that protect what matters most. Not legalism. Structure. Guardrails for love. We understand this in every important area of life.

Healthy marriages require rhythms.

Healthy parenting requires rhythms.

Healthy bodies require rhythms.

Healthy souls do too.

Without rhythms, important things drift. Prayer becomes sporadic. Scripture becomes occasional. Worship becomes reactive. Rest becomes neglected. And over time, what was central becomes peripheral. This is why structure matters. Not because structure creates life. But because it protects space for life.

A simple rule of life may include daily prayer, daily Scripture, weekly Sabbath, regular confession, regular silence, and intentional generosity. Not because God demands a system. But because love requires room. And room rarely appears accidentally. It is made intentionally. If you want to live near God, build your life to support nearness.

### Pre-Decide

One of the most practical tools that has helped me came from Craig Groeschel: Pre-decide. Decide beforehand.[9] Do not wait for temptation to make your choices. Make them before temptation arrives. This has been deeply helpful in my life. Because we all know our vulnerabilities. Our triggers. Our weak places. Our recurring lies.

I have identified some of the false stories I tell myself. And I have prepared responses. Solutions. Interruptions. Not perfectly. I do not always win. But now I win more than I lose. That matters. Growth is not perfection. It is progress. And progress often begins with preparation.

### Small Decisions Shape Big Destinies

Most people think spiritual collapse happens in dramatic moments. But usually it begins in small decisions. Neglected prayer. Compromised thought life. Unchecked bitterness. Quiet pride. Unconfessed sin. Drift is rarely sudden. It is cumulative.

This is why small decisions matter so much. The daily yes. The daily no. The small surrender. The small obedience. The unseen decision. These shape who we become. Character is not built in crisis. It is revealed there.

---

[9] Craig Groeschel, "Pre-Decide," YouTube video, posted by Life.Church, January 30, 2022, https://www.youtube.com/watch?v=fTHNRncZFKg

It is built in ordinary decisions long before the crisis arrives. Daniel did not become courageous in Babylon overnight. He had already formed convictions before the pressure came. Joseph did not suddenly become faithful in temptation. Faithfulness had already been formed. This is why pre-deciding matters.

We are shaping our future selves with present decisions. Every repeated yes to God strengthens future obedience. Every repeated surrender deepens future sensitivity. Small obediences create strong disciples. Never underestimate the power of ordinary faithfulness. God often builds extraordinary lives through ordinary obedience.

**Obedience Over Ease**

One of the defining mottos of our family remains: God has not called us to what is easy. He has called us to obedience. That truth has shaped our home. And it must shape our lives. The presence of God rarely leads us into convenience.

It leads us into faithfulness. Obedience is often costly. It interrupts comfort. Challenges preference. Exposes idols. But obedience keeps us near. And nearness is worth everything. To quote my friend, Roy Rhodes,

"Others may. I may not."

"Others can. I cannot."[10]

---

[10] Roy Rhodes, "The Danger of Zion," sermon, Illinois District Council, May 26, 2023, YouTube, https://www.youtube.com/watch?v=fEbzkQhTLkY.

Not because I am better. But because I belong. Nearness changes what feels permissible. Love changes what feels desirable. In John 15, Jesus gives the clearest invitation of all: "Abide in Me." This is the anchor of the Christian life. Fellowship with God is not merely visitation; it is abiding. It means staying, remaining, and rooting our lives in Him.

### Do Not Leave Your Spiritual Life to Chance

This may be the most important warning I can give: Do not leave your spiritual life to chance. Do not drift. Do not assume tomorrow. Do not delay surrender. Do not wait for another season. Another moment. Another opportunity. You are not guaranteed another opportunity.

If the Holy Spirit is prompting you—even now—respond. Take the cue. Take the hint. Start today. Do not choose ease over obedience. The enemy of your soul wants passivity. Compromise. Mediocrity. Resignation. Quit. Settle. Numb yourself. Drift.

But the Spirit calls you upward. Nearer. Closer. Deeper. Call on Him. Rely on Him. Yield to Him. He will help you.

### The Long Obedience of Presence

Much of spiritual life is less dramatic than people expect. It is not always revival moments. Breakthrough moments. Mountaintop moments. Often it is ordinary.

Quiet.

Repeated.

Hidden.

This is where many believers become discouraged. They expect constant intensity. Constant emotional confirmation. Constant visible growth. But formation is often slow.

Like roots.

Like seasons.

Like growth beneath the surface. And much of becoming a person of God's presence happens in hidden faithfulness. Showing up.

Praying again. Reading again. Repenting again. Trusting again. Returning again.

This is not failure. This is formation. Presence is not sustained by intensity. It is sustained by constancy. A long obedience in the same direction. Day after day. Year after year. And over time, what once felt intentional becomes natural.

Prayer becomes reflex. Worship becomes instinct. Obedience becomes joy. Awareness becomes normal. That is the beauty of long faithfulness. Not perfection. Formation. And often, we do not realize how deeply God has shaped us until we look back. And see who we once were. And who, by grace, we are becoming.

**The Journey of Presence**

This book has been about presence. Not abstract theology. Living reality.

- God in the middle.
- Jesus in the mess.
- Presence over promise.
- Peace in the storm.
- Awareness in the home.
- Formation by the Spirit.
- Light for the neighborhood.

**The Final Invitation**

And now the question remains: Will you become a person of His presence? Not occasionally. Daily. Not simply emotionally. Devotionally. Not accidentally. Intentionally. God is nearer than you realize. More willing than you imagine. More present than you know. Draw near. Make room. Choose obedience. Cultivate awareness. Protect devotion. And become the kind of person who carries the presence of God into every room you enter.

Because the world does not merely need better Christians. It needs people of His presence.

**"I'll serve You, no bargaining. My life is my offering."**

The life you were made for has been waiting for you in the presence of God all along.

## Chapter 8 Reflection Guide

### Reflect

1. What patterns in my daily life are currently shaping the kind of person I am becoming?

2. Where have I become spiritually distracted, passive, or numb to God's presence?

3. What competing loves or priorities have dulled my awareness of God's nearness?

4. What practices help me stay attentive to the Holy Spirit—and which habits consistently pull me away?

5. If I continue living exactly as I am today, who will I become in five years?

---

### Respond

Choose one intentional practice of presence to strengthen starting today.

Examples:

- a daily prayer rhythm
- scheduled Scripture reading
- Sabbath rest
- reducing digital distraction

- setting prayer reminders
- pre-deciding your response to temptation
- creating space for silence and listening

Choose one.

Start now.

Do not wait.

Remember: You do not drift into God's presence. You draw near.

---

**Start Here**

Simple.

Tomorrow morning:

- begin with prayer
- open Scripture
- listen
- obey one thing

**Pray**

Lord,

thank You for inviting me into a life lived near You.

Forgive me for the ways I have drifted, delayed, or allowed other things to compete for my devotion.

Teach me to live aware of Your presence.

Help me become sensitive to Your Spirit and faithful in my choices.

Strengthen my devotion and deepen my hunger for You.

Give me courage to choose obedience over ease and surrender over distraction.

Shape me into the person You designed me to be.

Let my life reflect Your presence in every place I go.

And by Your Spirit, make me more like Jesus every day.

In Jesus' name, amen.

# EPILOGUE: A Final Word

If you have made it this far, thank you. Not merely for reading these words, but for taking seriously the deeper invitation beneath them. Because this book was never merely about ideas. It was about invitation.

An invitation into the life you were made for. A life not built on hurry, achievement, image, or accumulation. A life built on presence. God's presence. If there is one thing I hope you carry with you after these pages, it is this: God is nearer than you think.

He has always been nearer than you think. In your victories. In your failures. In your questions. In your waiting. In your grief. In your joy. In your home. In your calling. In the hidden places. In the ordinary places. In the painful places.

He is there.

And He is not waiting for a polished version of you. He is not waiting for you to become impressive. He is not waiting for you to get it all together. He is inviting you now. As you are. Into deeper communion. Into deeper surrender. Into deeper formation.

The Christian life is not built in giant moments alone. It is built in daily returning. Returning in prayer. Returning in Scripture. Returning in repentance. Returning in worship. Returning in trust. Again. And again. And again.

Not because God keeps leaving. But because we keep wandering. And still, He welcomes us back. That is grace. The world is loud. Fast. Demanding. Distracting. And if you are not intentional, it will disciple you. It will shape your desires. Shape your pace. Shape your loves.

But you do not have to be shaped by the world around you. You can be shaped by the Spirit within you. You can become a person of His presence. Not perfectly. But faithfully. And when you do, you will find something extraordinary: Peace that does not collapse under pressure. Joy that survives suffering. Love that outlasts offense. Faithfulness that remains. Light that shines in darkness.

Not because you became stronger. But because you stayed near. So before you move on—before you return to your routines, your responsibilities, your unfinished tasks—pause here for a moment. Ask yourself: What is God saying to me? What needs to change? What needs to be surrendered? What needs to be reordered? What needs to be healed? And perhaps most importantly: What would it look like for me to live tomorrow with deeper awareness of God than I did today?

Start there.

Not next year. Not when life slows down. Not when things get easier. Start now. Because the life you were made for is not somewhere far away. It begins with the next yes. The next prayer. The next act of surrender. The next moment of attention.

And as you walk forward, remember: You are not walking alone. The God who called you is with you. The Spirit who formed you is in you. And the Christ who saved you walks before you. Stay near Him. And in staying near Him, become who you were always meant to be.

Grace and peace,

— **Brandon D. Arneson**

# Study Guide

Reflect. Respond. Practice. Pray

**How to Use This Guide**

This guide can be used personally, with your family, or in a group setting. Move slowly. Be honest. Do not rush to answers. The goal is not information, but transformation.

Read each chapter prayerfully. Revisit the Scriptures. Reflect honestly. Respond practically. Practice intentionally. Pray sincerely.

Remember: the goal of this book is not merely to learn about the presence of God, but to live in it.

## Chapter 1

## God in the Middle

### Reflect

1. Where in your life have you felt “in the middle”—uncertain, unresolved, or displaced?

2. What part of Jacob’s story feels most relatable to your own journey?

3. How have you seen God meet you in unexpected places?

### Respond

4. What are you currently running from, avoiding, or trying to control?

5. What would surrender look like in your present season?

### Practice

6. Set aside ten minutes this week to reflect on where God has been present in difficult seasons of your life.

### Pray

7. Ask God to open your eyes to His presence in places you have overlooked.

## Chapter 2

## Jesus in the Mess

### Reflect

1. Where have you looked for satisfaction apart from Christ?

2. What wells have you returned to that have left you thirsty?

3. What does the Samaritan woman's story teach you about grace?

### Respond

4. What shame are you still carrying that Jesus may be confronting?

5. What part of your story needs healing?

### Practice

6. Write your testimony in three parts: before Christ, meeting Christ, life with Christ.

### Pray

7. Ask Jesus to meet you honestly and heal what still hurts.

## Chapter 3

### Presence Over Promise

#### Reflect

1. What "promised lands" tempt you to value blessing over God Himself?

2. Have you ever wanted what God could give more than God Himself?

3. What does Moses teach us about priority?

#### Respond

4. Where has comfort become more important than communion?

5. What needs to be reordered in your heart?

#### Practice

6. Spend one prayer time this week asking for nothing—simply enjoying God's presence.

#### Pray

7. Ask God to deepen your desire for Him, not merely His gifts.

## Chapter 4

## Shalom Reigning

### Reflect

1. How do you normally define peace?
2. What currently threatens your peace?
3. What does biblical peace look like in your life?

### Respond

4. What anxieties have been ruling your thoughts?
5. What would it mean to let Christ rule your inner life?

### Practice

6. Identify one recurring anxious thought and intentionally surrender it to God each day.

### Pray

7. Ask Christ to establish His peace deeply in your soul.

## Chapter 5

## Good News for My Family

### Reflect

1. What rhythms currently shape your home?

2. What spiritual atmosphere exists in your household?

3. What have your children (or those closest to you) learned by watching you?

### Respond

4. What needs to change in your household rhythms?

5. Where has ease become more important than obedience?

### Practice

6. Create one new household rhythm this week (prayer, Scripture, Sabbath, worship).

### Pray

7. Ask God to make His presence tangible in your home.

## Chapter 6

## Formed by the Spirit

### Reflect

1. How has the Holy Spirit corrected you recently?

2. Where are you resisting His shaping work?

3. Which fruit of the Spirit needs development in your life?

### Respond

4. Are you pursuing gifts more than character?

5. Where do you need deeper surrender?

### Practice

6. Focus intentionally on one fruit of the Spirit this week.

### Pray

7. Ask the Holy Spirit to form Christ's character more deeply in you.

## Chapter 7

## Be Light

### Reflect

1. Who has God placed in your path right now?
2. How do you currently see your neighbors?
3. What does it mean to be light where you are?

### Respond

4. Where have you been inattentive to people around you?
5. What fears keep you from witnessing?

### Practice

6. Pray for and engage one person intentionally this week.

### Pray

7. Ask God for eyes to see and courage to speak.

## Chapter 8

## Becoming People of His Presence

### Reflect

1. What most distracts you from awareness of God?

2. What practices most help you stay near Him?

3. What has God been saying to you through this book?

### Respond

4. What needs to be reordered in your daily life?

5. What is your next step of obedience?

### Practice

6. Build a personal "presence plan" for the next 30 days (prayer, Scripture, worship, Sabbath).

### Pray

7. Ask God to deepen your awareness of His nearness and strengthen your devotion.

**Final Group Question**

What is one thing God has changed in you through this journey?

**Final Personal Question**

What would it look like to live tomorrow with deeper awareness of God than you did today?

You may find this useful for small groups or family discussions.

# Bibliography

Augustine of Hippo. *Confessions*, Book I.

Brueggemann, Walter. *Sabbath as Resistance: Saying No to the Culture of Now*. John Knox Press, 2017.

Fee, Gordon. *Paul, the Spirit, and the People of God*. Baker Academics, 2023.

Foster, Richard. *Celebration of Discipline: The Path to Spiritual Growth*. HarperSanFransico, 2018.

Groeschel, Craig. "Pre-Decide." YouTube video. Posted by Life.Church. January 30, 2022. https://www.youtube.com/watch?v=fTHNRncZFKg.

Keller, Timothy. *Generous Justice: How God's Grace Make Us Just*. Dutton, 2010.

Lawrence, Brother. *The practice of the presence of God: The complete works of Brother Lawrence with notes and Scripture references*. Perieco Publishing, 2009.

Rhodes, Roy. "The Danger of Zion." Sermon. Illinois District Council. May 26, 2023. YouTube. https://www.youtube.com/watch?v=fEbzkQhTLkY.

Tozer, A.W. *The Pursuit of God*. Christian Publications, Inc, 1948.

Willard, Dallas. *Renovation of the Heart: Putting on the Character of Christ*. NavPress, 2021.

# About the Author

Brandon D. Arneson has served in Christian ministry for more than two decades and currently serves as Lead Pastor of city.light church in DeKalb, Illinois. Before pastoring in DeKalb, Brandon and his family served as missionaries in Nepal, where they ministered in church planting, leadership development, and compassionate care ministry in challenging environments.

Brandon holds a Bachelor of Arts from Central Bible College and a Master of Arts from Trinity Bible College and Graduate School and is currently pursuing his Doctor of Ministry at Assemblies of God Theological Seminary. He is passionate about spiritual formation, Sabbath rhythms, healthy leadership, and helping people build lives deeply rooted in the presence of God.

Brandon and his wife, Bethany, have been married for over twenty years and are raising seven children together. Whether pastoring, teaching, writing, or parenting, his greatest desire is to help people discover the life they were made for: life in the presence of God.

www.ingramcontent.com/pod-product-compliance
Lightning Source LLC
LaVergne TN
LVHW010621100826
845148LV00014B/3055
* 9 7 9 8 2 3 4 0 8 3 1 7 3 *